To

From

Date

PROMISES & PRAYERS

for Friends

SECOND EDITION

PROMISES & PRAYERS

for Friends

FAMILY CHRISTIAN PRESS
Grand Rapids, MI 49530

The quoted ideas expressed in this book (but not scripture verses) are not, in all cases, exact quotations, as some have been edited for clarity and brevity. In all cases, the author has attempted to maintain the speaker's original intent. In some cases, quoted material for this book was obtained from secondary sources, primarily print media. While every effort was made to ensure the accuracy of these sources, the accuracy cannot be guaranteed. For additions, deletions, corrections or clarifications in future editions of this text, please write FAMILY CHRISTIAN PRESS.

Cover Design by Kim Russell / Wahoo Designs
Page Layout by Bart Dawson

ISBN 1-58334-239-7

Printed in the United States of America

FAMILY
CHRISTIAN
PRESS

Table of Contents

Introduction

Loyal friendship is ordained by God. Throughout the Bible, we are reminded to care for one another, and to treat one another as we wish to be treated. The familiar words of 1 Corinthians 13:13 remind us that love and charity are among God's greatest gifts: "But now faith, hope, love, abide these three; but the greatest of these is love" (NASB).

This text is a celebration of friendship that addresses 72 topics of intense interest to Christians. Each brief chapter contains Bible verses, a quotation, and a prayer. The ideas in each chapter are powerful reminders of God's commandments and reminders of the joys that accompany Christian friendship.

Concentration camp survivor Corrie ten Boom observed, "The glory of friendship is not the outstretched hand, or the kindly smile, or the joy of companionship. It is the spiritual inspiration that comes to one when he discovers that someone else believes in him and is willing to trust him with his friendship." These words remind us that enduring friendships between likeminded believers are blessed gifts from above. Today and every day, may we give thanks for those gifts and make them grow.

Abundance

My cup runs over. Surely goodness and mercy shall follow me all the days of my life; and I will dwell in the house of the Lord forever.

Psalm 23:5, 6 NKJV

Now this I say, he who sows sparingly will also reap sparingly, and he who sows bountifully will also reap bountifully.

2 Corinthians 9:6 NASB

If you give, you will receive. Your gift will return to you in full measure, pressed down, shaken together to make room for more, and running over. Whatever measure you use in giving—large or small—it will be used to measure what is given back to you.

Luke 6:38 NLT

His lord said unto him, Well done, thou good and faithful servant: thou hast been faithful over a few things, I will make thee ruler over many things: enter thou into the joy of thy lord.

Matthew 25:21 KJV

The 10th chapter of John tells us that Christ came to earth so that our lives might be filled with abundance. But what, exactly, did Jesus mean when He promised "life . . . more abundantly?" Was He referring to material possessions or financial wealth? Hardly. Jesus offers a different kind of abundance: a spiritual richness that extends beyond the temporal boundaries of this world. This everlasting abundance is available to all who seek it and claim it. May we, as believers, claim the riches of Christ Jesus every day that we live, and may we share His blessings with our families, with our friends, and with all who cross our path.

People, places, and things were never
meant to give us life.
God alone is the author of a fulfilling life.

Gary Smalley and John Trent

— A Prayer —

Father, thank You for the joyful, abundant life that is mine through Christ Jesus. Guide me according to Your will, and help me to be a loyal friend to others through all that I say and do. Give me courage, Lord, to claim the spiritual riches that You have promised, and lead me according to Your plan for my life, today and always.

Amen

Accepting Christ

I will be your God throughout your lifetime—until your hair is white with age. I made you, and I will care for you. I will carry you along and save you.

Isaiah 46:4 NLT

The LORD is my strength and my song; he has become my salvation. He is my God, and I will praise him, my father's God, and I will exalt him.

Exodus 15:2 NIV

For God so loved the world, that he gave his only begotten Son, that whosoever believeth in him should not perish, but have everlasting life.

John 3:16 KJV

Jesus answered and said unto her, Whosoever drinketh of this water shall thirst again: but whosoever drinketh of the water that I shall give him shall never thirst; but the water that I shall give him shall be in him a well of water springing up into everlasting life.

John 4:13, 14 KJV

God loves you. Period. And His affection for you is deeper and more profound than you can imagine. God's love for you is so great that He sent His only Son to this earth to die for your sins and to offer you the priceless gift of eternal life. Now, you must decide whether or not to accept God's gift. Will you ignore it or embrace it? Will you return it or neglect it? Will you accept Christ or not? The decision, of course, is yours and yours alone, and the decision has eternal consequences. Accept God's gift: Accept Christ today.

To accept Christ is to know the meaning of the words "as he is, so are we in this world." We accept his friends as our friends, his enemies as our enemies, his ways as our ways, his rejection as our rejection, his cross as our cross, his life as our life, and his future as our future.

A. W. Tozer

— A Prayer —

Dear Lord, You sent Your Son to this earth that we might have the gift of eternal life. Thank You, Father, for that priceless gift. Help me to share the wondrous message of Jesus with my family and friends so that they, too, might accept Him as their Savior. And, let me praise You always for the new life You have given me, a life that is both abundant and eternal.

Amen

Anger

Don't become angry quickly, because getting angry is foolish.

Ecclesiastes 7:9 NCV

"A patient man has great understanding,
but a quick-tempered man displays folly."

Proverbs 14:29 NIV

My dearly loved brothers, understand this:
everyone must be quick to hear, slow to speak,
and slow to anger, for man's anger does not
accomplish God's righteousness.

James 1-19, 20 HCSB

"Make no friendship with an angry man . . . ."

Proverbs 22:24 KJV

When you are angry, do not sin,
and be sure to stop being angry before the end of the day.
Do not give the devil a way to defeat you.

Ephesians 4:26, 27 NCV

Your temper is either your master or your servant. Either you control it, or it controls you. And the extent to which you allow anger to rule your life will determine, to a surprising extent, the quality of your relationships with others and your relationship with God.

Anger and peace cannot coexist in the same mind. If you allow yourself to be chronically angry, you must forfeit, albeit temporarily, the peace that might otherwise be yours through Christ. So obey God's Word by turning away from anger today and every day. You'll be glad you did, and so will your family and friends.

Bitterness and anger, usually over trivial things, make havoc of homes, churches, and friendships.

Warren Wiersbe

— A Prayer —

Lord, I can be so impatient, and I can become so angry. Calm me down, Lord, and give me the maturity and the wisdom to be a patient, forgiving Christian friend. Just as You have forgiven me, Father, let me forgive others so that I can follow the example of Your Son.

Amen

Anxiety

Be anxious for nothing, but in everything by prayer
and supplication with thanksgiving
let your requests be made known to God.

Philippians 4:6 NASB

Anxiety in the heart of man causes depression,
but a good word makes it glad.

Proverbs 12:25 NKJV

Therefore I tell you, do not worry about your life,
what you will eat or drink; or about your body,
what you will wear. Is life not more important than food
and the body more important than clothes?
Look at the birds of the air; they do not sow or reap
or store away in barns, and yet your heavenly father
feeds them. Are you not much more valuable than they?
Who of you by worrying can add a single hour to his life?

Matthew 6:25, 27 NIV

God is our refuge and strength,
a very present help in trouble.

Psalm 46:1 KJV

We live in a world that sometimes seems to shift beneath our feet. From time to time, all of us face adversity, discouragement, or disappointment. And, throughout life, we must all endure life-changing personal losses that leave us breathless. When we do, God stands ready to protect us. Psalm 147 promises, "He heals the brokenhearted, and binds their wounds" (v. 3 NIV). Does your world seem to be trembling beneath your feet? Seek protection from the One who cannot be moved. The same God who created the universe will protect you if you ask Him . . . so ask Him.

One of the main missions of God is to free us from the debilitating bonds of fear and anxiety. God's heart is broken when He sees us so demoralized and weighed down by fear.

Bill Hybels

— A Prayer —

Lord, sometimes this world is a difficult place, and, as a frail human being, I am fearful. When I am anxious, turn my thoughts to You. When I grieve, touch my heart with Your enduring love. And, keep me mindful, Lord, that nothing, absolutely nothing, will happen this day that You and I cannot handle together.

Amen

Asking God

And yet the reason you don't have what you want is that you don't ask God for it.

James 4:2 NLT

So I say to you, keep asking, and it will be given to you. Keep searching, and you will find. Keep knocking, and the door will be opened to you.

Luke 11:9 HCSB

Until now you have not asked for anything in my name. Ask and you will receive, so that your joy will be the fullest possible joy.

John 16:24 NCV

Verily, verily, I say unto you, He that believeth on me, the works that I do shall he do also; and greater works than these shall he do; because I go unto my Father. And whatsoever ye shall ask in my name, that will I do, that the Father may be glorified in the Son. If ye shall ask any thing in my name, I will do it.

John 14:12-14 KJV

Sometimes, amid the demands and the frustrations of everyday life, we forget to slow ourselves down long enough to talk with God. Instead of turning our thoughts and prayers to Him, we rely upon our own resources. Instead of praying for strength and courage, we seek to manufacture it within ourselves. Instead of asking God for guidance, we depend only upon our own limited wisdom. The results of such behaviors are unfortunate and, on occasion, tragic.

Are you in need? Ask God to sustain you. Are you troubled? Take your worries to Him in prayer. Are you weary? Seek God's strength. In all things great and small, seek God's wisdom and His grace. He hears your prayers, and He will answer. All you must do is ask.

There is a communion with God that asks for nothing, yet asks for everything . . . He who seeks the Father more than anything he can give is likely to have what he asks, for he is not likely to ask amiss.

George MacDonald

— A Prayer —

Lord, You are the giver of all things good.
When I am in need, let me come to You in prayer.
You know the desires of my heart, Lord;
grant them, I ask. Yet not my will, Father,
but Your will be done.

Amen

Attitude

A miserable heart means a miserable life;
a cheerful heart fills the day with a song.

Proverbs 15:15 MSG

Set your mind on the things above,
not on the things that are on earth.

Colossians 3:2 NASB

Your attitude should be the same as that of Christ Jesus: Who, being in very nature God, did not consider equality with God something to be grasped, but made himself nothing, taking the very nature of a servant, being made in human likeness. And being found in appearance as a man, he humbled himself and became obedient to death— even death on a cross!

Philippians 2:5-8 NIV

Finally, brethren, whatever things are true, whatever things are noble, whatever things are just, whatever things are pure, whatever things are lovely, whatever things are of good report, if there is any virtue and if there is anything praiseworthy—meditate on these things.

Philippians 4:8 NKJV

What's your attitude today? Are you fearful, angry, bored, or worried? Are you worried more about pleasing your friends than about pleasing your God? Are you confused, bitter, or pessimistic? If so, God wants to have a little talk with you.

God wants you to experience joy and abundance, but He will not force His joy upon you; you must claim it for yourself. So today, and every day thereafter, celebrate this life that God has given you. Think optimistically about yourself and your future. Give thanks to the One who has given you everything, and trust in your heart that He wants to give you so much more.

Do you feel the world is treating you well? If your attitude toward the world is excellent, you will receive excellent results. If you feel so-so about the world, your response from that world will be average. If you feel badly about your world, you will seem to have only negative feedback from life.

John Maxwell

— A Prayer —

Dear Lord, let me live my life and love my friends with a spirit of hope and thanksgiving. And, let me show my friends—by my words and my deeds—that the Christian life is a life of optimism and trust. Whatever circumstances I face, whether good or bad, triumphal or tragic, let my response reflect a God-honoring, Christlike attitude of faith and love for You.

Amen

Behavior

Therefore, get your minds ready for action, being self-disciplined, and set your hope completely on the grace to be brought to you at the revelation of Jesus Christ. As obedient children, do not be conformed to the desires of your former ignorance but, as the One who called you is holy, you also are to be holy in all your conduct.

1 Peter 1:13-15 HCSB

Walk in a manner worthy of the God who calls you into His own kingdom and glory.

1 Thessalonians 2:12 NASB

"Teach me your ways, O Lord, that I may live according to your truth! Grant me purity of heart, that I may honor you."

Psalm 86:11 NLT

"For the Lord God is our light and our protector. He gives us grace and glory. No good thing will the Lord withhold from those who do what is right. O Lord Almighty, happy are those who trust in you."

Psalm 84:11, 12 NLT

Life is a series of decisions and choices. Each day, we make countless decisions that can bring us closer to God . . . or not. When we live according to God's commandments, we earn for ourselves the abundance and peace that He intends for our lives. But, when we turn our backs upon God by disobeying Him, we bring needless suffering upon ourselves and our families.

Do you seek God's peace and His blessings? Then obey Him. When you're faced with a difficult choice or a powerful temptation, seek God's counsel and trust the counsel He gives. Invite God into your heart and live according to His commandments. When you do, you will be blessed today, and tomorrow, and forever.

More depends on my walk than my talk.

D. L. Moody

— A Prayer —

Lord, it is so much easier to speak of the righteous life
than it is to live it. Let me live righteously,
and let my actions be consistent with my beliefs.
Let every step that I take reflect Your truth,
and let me live a life that is worthy of Your Son.

Amen

Born Again

Jesus answered and said to him,
"Truly, truly, I say to you, unless one is born again
he cannot see the kingdom of God."

John 3:3 NASB

Blessed be the God and Father of our Lord Jesus Christ, who according to His great mercy has caused us to be born again to a living hope through the resurrection of Jesus Christ from the dead.

1 Peter 1:3 NASB

For it is by grace you have been saved, through faith— and this not from yourselves, it is the gift of God . . . .

Ephesians 2:8 NIV

For God sent not his Son into the world to condemn the world; but that the world through him might be saved.

John 3:17 KJV

These things have I written unto you that believe on the name of the Son of God;
that ye may know that ye have eternal life . . . .

1 John 5:13 KJV

Christ sacrificed His life on the cross so that we might be born again. This gift, freely given from God's only begotten Son, is the priceless possession of everyone who accepts Him as Lord and Savior.

God is waiting patiently for each of us to accept the gift of eternal life. Let us claim Christ's gift today. Let us walk with the Savior, let us love Him, let us praise Him, and let us share His message of salvation with the world.

Jesus divided people—everyone—into two classes—
the once-born and the twice-born, the unconverted
and the converted. No other distinction mattered.

E. Stanley Jones

— A Prayer —

Lord, when I accepted Jesus as my personal savior,
You changed me forever and made me whole.
I was born again. Help me to share Your Son's message
with my friends. You are a God of love,
redemption, conversion, and salvation.
I will praise You today and forever.

Amen

Cheerfulness

Jacob said, "For what a relief it is to see your friendly smile. It is like seeing the smile of God!"

Genesis 33:10 NLT

Worry is a heavy load, but a kind word cheers you up.

Proverbs 12:25 NCV

I will thank you, Lord with all my heart;
I will tell of all the marvelous things you have done.
I will be filled with joy because of you.
I will sing praises to your name, O Most High.

Psalm 9:1, 2 NLT

I will praise the name of God with a song,
and will magnify him with thanksgiving.

Psalm 69:30 KJV

Set your mind on the things above,
not on the things that are on earth.

Colossians 3:2 NASB

Cheerfulness is a gift that we give to others and to ourselves. And, as believers who have been saved by a risen Christ, why shouldn't we be cheerful? The answer, of course, is that we have every reason to honor our Savior with joy in our hearts, smiles on our faces, and words of celebration on our lips.

Are you a cheerful Christian? You should be! And what is the best way to receive from Christ the joy that is rightfully yours? By giving Him what is rightfully His: your heart, your soul, and your life.

When I think of God, my heart is so full of joy that the notes leap and dance as they leave my pen; and since God has given me a cheerful heart, I serve him with a cheerful spirit.

Franz Joseph Haydn

— A Prayer —

Dear Lord, make me a cheerful friend to all whom I meet. Your Holy Word reminds me that this is the day that You have created; let me rejoice in it. Today, let me choose an attitude of celebration. Let me be quick to smile and slow to anger. And, let Your love shine in me and through me.

Amen

Conscience

I will maintain my righteousness and never let go of it; my conscience will not reproach me as long as I live.

Job 27:6 NIV

For indeed, the kingdom of God is within you.

Luke 17:21 NKJV

And do not be conformed to this world, but be transformed by the renewing of your mind, that you may prove what is that good and acceptable and perfect will of God.

Romans 12:2 NKJV

This being so, I myself always strive to have a conscience without offense toward God and men.

Acts 24:16 NKJV

Let us come near to God with a sincere heart and a sure faith, because we have been made free from a guilty conscience, and our bodies have been washed with pure water.

Hebrews 10:22 NCV

Few things in life torment us more than a guilty conscience. And, few things in life provide more contentment than the knowledge that we are obeying God's commandments. A clear conscience is one of the rewards we earn when we obey God's Word and follow His will. When we follow God's will and accept His gift of salvation, our earthly rewards are never-ceasing, and our heavenly rewards are everlasting.

A quiet conscience sleeps in thunder.

Thomas Fuller

— A Prayer —

Lord, You have given me a conscience that tells me right from wrong. Let me listen to that quiet voice so that I might do Your will and follow Your Word today and every day.

Amen

Courage

*Be strong and brave, and do the work.
Don't be afraid or discouraged, because the Lord God,
my God, is with you. He will not fail you or leave you.*

1 Chronicles 28:20 NCV

Watch, stand fast in the faith, be brave, be strong.

1 Corinthians 16:13 NKJV

*The Lord is my light and my salvation; whom shall I fear?
The Lord is the strength of my life; of whom shall I be afraid?*

Psalm 27:1 KJV

*But Jesus beheld them, and said unto them,
"With men this is impossible;
but with God all things are possible."*

Matthew 19:26 KJV

*In thee, O Lord, do I put my trust;
let me never be put into confusion.*

Psalm 71:1 KJV

Because we are saved by a risen Christ, we can have hope for the future, no matter how desperate our circumstances may seem. After all, God has promised that we are His throughout eternity. And, He has told us that we must place our hopes in Him.

Today, summon the courage to follow God. Even if the path seems difficult, even if your heart is fearful, trust your Heavenly Father and follow Him. Trust Him with your day and your life. Do His work, care for His children, and share His Good News. Let Him guide your steps. He will not lead you astray.

Our Lord is searching for people who
will make a difference. Christians dare not
dissolve into the background or
blend into the neutral scenery of the world.

Charles Swindoll

— A Prayer —

Dear Lord, sometimes this world is a fearful place.
I fear for my family and my friends. Yet,
You have promised that You are with us always.
With You as our protector, I am not afraid.
Today, Dear Lord, let me live courageously
as I place my trust in You.

Amen

Encouraging Others

So encourage each other and give each other strength, just as you are doing now.

1 Thessalonians 5:11 NCV

Encourage each other. Live in harmony and peace. Then the God of love and peace will be with you.

2 Corinthians 13:11 NLT

But encourage one another day after day, as long as it is still called "Today," so that none of you will be hardened by the deceitfulness of sin.

Hebrews 3:13 NASB

Feed the flock of God which is among you . . . .

1 Peter 5:2 KJV

Be kindly affectioned one to another with brotherly love; in honor preferring one another; not slothful in business; fervent in spirit; serving the Lord; rejoicing in hope; patient in tribulation; continuing instant in prayer . . . .

Romans 12:10-12 KJV

The words that we speak have the power to do great good or great harm. If we speak words of encouragement and hope, we can lift others up. And that's exactly what God commands us to do!

God intends that we speak words of kindness, wisdom, and truth, no matter our circumstances, no matter our emotions. When we do, we share a priceless gift with the world, and we give glory to the One who gave His life for us. As believers, we must do no less.

We can never untangle all the woes in other people's lives. We can't produce miracles overnight. But we can bring a cup of cool water to a thirsty soul, or a scoop of laughter to a lonely heart.

Barbara Johnson

— A Prayer —

Dear Lord, You have loved me eternally, and cared for me faithfully. Just as You have lifted me up, Lord, let me also lift up others in a spirit of encouragement, optimism, and hope. Today and every day, let me share Your healing message so that I might encourage others. And, Lord, may the glory be Yours.

Amen

Eternal Life

Behold, I tell you a mystery; we will not all sleep, but we will all be changed, in a moment, in the twinkling of an eye, at the last trumpet; for the trumpet will sound, and the dead will be raised imperishable, and we will be changed. For this perishable must put on the imperishable, and this mortal must put on immortality. But when this perishable will have put on the imperishable, and this mortal will have put on immortality, then will come about the saying that is written, "DEATH IS SWALLOWED UP IN VICTORY. "O DEATH, WHERE IS YOUR VICTORY? O DEATH, WHERE IS YOUR STING?" *The sting of death is sin, and the power of sin is the law; but thanks be to God, who gives us the victory through our Lord Jesus Christ.*

1 Corinthians 15:51–57 NASB

Because I live, you will live also.

Jesus
John 14:19 NASB

Jesus answered and said unto her, Whosoever drinketh of this water shall thirst again: but whosoever drinketh of the water that I shall give him shall never thirst; but the water that I shall give him shall be in him a well of water springing up into everlasting life.

John 4:13, 14 KJV

Christ sacrificed His life on the cross so that we might have eternal life. This gift, freely given by God's only begotten Son, is the priceless possession of everyone who accepts Him as Lord and Savior. God is waiting patiently for each of us to accept the gift of eternal life. Let us claim Christ's gift today.

May we, who have been given so much, praise our Savior for the gift of eternal life, and may we share the joyous news of our Master's love and His grace.

Teach us to set our hopes on heaven, to hold firmly to the promise of eternal life, so that we can withstand the struggles and storms of this world.

Max Lucado

— A Prayer —

Lord, I am only here on this earth for a brief while. But, You have offered me the priceless gift of eternal life through Your Son Jesus. I accept Your gift, Lord, with thanksgiving and praise. Let me share the good news of my salvation with those who need Your healing touch.

Amen

Failures

Therefore if any man be in Christ, he is a new creature:
old things are passed away;
behold, all things are become new.

2 Corinthians 5:17 KJV

Weeping may endure for a night,
but joy cometh in the morning.

Psalm 30:5 KJV

Have mercy on me, O God, according to your unfailing love; according to your great compassion blot out my transgressions. Wash away all my iniquity and cleanse me from my sin.

Psalm 51:1, 2 NIV

If we confess our sins, he is faithful and just and will forgive us our sins and purify us from all unrighteousness.

1 John 1:9 NIV

I will instruct you and teach you in the way you should go;
I will counsel you and watch over you.

Psalm 32:8 NIV

The occasional disappointments and failures of life are inevitable. Such setbacks are simply the price that we must occasionally pay for our willingness to take risks as we follow our dreams. But even when we encounter bitter disappointments, we must never lose faith.

When we call upon God in heartfelt prayer, He will answer—in His own time and according to His own plan—and He will heal us. And, while we are waiting for God's plans to unfold and for His healing touch to restore us, we can be comforted in the knowledge that our Creator can overcome any obstacle, even if we cannot.

Maturity in Christ is about consistent pursuit in spite of the attacks and setbacks. It is about remaining in the arms of God. Abiding and staying, even in my weakness, even in my failure.

Angela Thomas

— A Prayer —

Lord, sometimes I make mistakes and fall short of Your commandments. When I do, forgive me, Father. And help me learn from my mistakes so that I can be a better servant to You and a better example to my friends and family.

Amen

Faith

It is impossible to please God apart from faith. And why? Because anyone who wants to approach God must believe both that he exists and that he cares enough to respond to those who seek him.

Hebrews 1:6 MSG

Now the just shall live by faith.

Hebrews 10:38 NKJV

If you have faith as a mustard seed, you shall say to this mountain, "Move from here to there" and it shall move; and nothing shall be impossible to you.

Matthew 17:20 NASB

The Lord's lovingkindnesses indeed never cease, for His compassions never fail. They are new every morning. Great is Thy faithfulness.

Lamentations 3:22, 23 NASB

For in the gospel a righteousness is being revealed, a righteousness that is by faith from first to last, just as it is written: "The righteous will live by faith."

Romans 1:17 NIV

Every life—including yours—is a series of successes and failures, celebrations and disappointments, joys and sorrows. Every step of the way, through every triumph and tragedy, God will stand by your side and strengthen you . . . if you have faith in Him. Jesus taught His disciples that if they had faith, they could move mountains. You can too.

When you place your faith, your trust, indeed your life in the hands of Christ Jesus, you'll be amazed at the marvelous things He can do with you and through you. With Him, all things are possible, and He stands ready to open a world of possibilities to you . . . if you have faith.

Hope must be in the future tense.
Faith, to be faith, must always be in the present tense.

Catherine Marshall

— A Prayer —

Heavenly Father, Your faithfulness is complete
and perfect. Great is Your faithfulness.
Lord, help me to be faithful to You,
and to demonstrate faithfulness
and loyalty to my friends.

Amen

Forgiveness

Be gentle with one another, sensitive. Forgive one another as quickly and thoroughly as God in Christ forgave you.

Ephesians 4:32 MSG

And whenever you stand praying, if you have anything against anyone, forgive him, so that your Father in heaven may also forgive you your wrongdoing.

Mark 11:25 HCSB

Then came Peter to him, and said, Lord, how oft shall my brother sin against me, and I forgive him? till seven times? Jesus saith unto him, I say not unto thee, Until seven times: but, Until seventy times seven.

Matthew 18:21, 22 KJV

So in everything, do to others what you would have them do to you, for this sums up the Law and the Prophets.

Matthew 7:12 NIV

Blessed are the merciful: for they shall obtain mercy.

Matthew 5:7 KJV

God's power to forgive, like His love, is infinite. Despite your shortcomings, despite your sins, God offers you immediate forgiveness and eternal life when you accept Christ as your Savior.

As a believer who is the recipient of God's forgiveness, how should you behave towards others? Should you forgive them (just as God has forgiven you) or should you remain embittered and resentful? The answer, of course, is found in God's Word: You are instructed to forgive others. When you do, you not only obey God's command, you also free yourself from a prison of your own making.

Our forgiveness toward others should flow from
a realization and appreciation of
God's forgiveness toward us.

Franklin Graham

— A Prayer —

Lord, make me a forgiving friend. When I am bitter, You can change my unforgiving heart. And, when I am slow to forgive, Your Word reminds me that forgiveness is Your commandment. Let me be Your obedient servant, Lord, and let me forgive others just as You have forgiven me.

Amen

Friendship

Beloved, if God so loved us,
we also ought to love one another.

1 John 4:11 NKJV

A friend loves at all times . . . .

Proverbs 17:17 NIV

How good and pleasant it is when
brothers live together in unity!

Psalm 133:1 NIV

Happy are those who deal justly with others
and always do what is right.

Psalm 106:3 NLT

As we have therefore opportunity,
let us do good unto all men . . . .

Galatians 6:10 KJV

How wonderful are the joys of friendship. Today, as you consider the many blessings that God has given you, remember to thank Him for the friends He has chosen to place along your path. May you be a blessing to them, and may they richly bless you today, tomorrow, and every day that you live.

We long to find someone who has been where
we've been, who shares our fragile skies,
who sees our sunsets with the same shades of blue.

Beth Moore

— *A Prayer* —

Thank You, Lord, for the Friend I have in Jesus. And, thank You for the dear friends You have given me, the friends who enrich my life. I pray for them today, and ask Your blessings upon them.

Amen

Generosity

God has given gifts to each of you from his great variety of spiritual gifts. Manage them well so that God's generosity can flow through you.

1 Peter 4:10 NLT

Each person should do as he has decided in his heart— not out of regret or out of necessity, for God loves a cheerful giver.

2 Corinthians 9:7 HCSB

He that hath two coats, let him impart to him that hath none; and he that hath meat, let him do likewise.

Luke 3:11 KJV

And let us not be weary in well doing: for in due season we shall reap, if we faint not.

Galatians 6:9 KJV

And above all things have fervent charity among yourselves: for charity shall cover the multitude of sins.

1 Peter 4:8 KJV

God is merciful and loving; God's gifts are beyond description; God's blessings are beyond comprehension; God has been incredibly generous with us, and He rightfully expects us to be generous with others.

Do you seek God's abundance and His peace? Then share the blessings that God has given you. Share your possessions, share your faith, share your testimony, and share your love. God expects no less, and He deserves no less. And neither, come to think of it, do your neighbors.

It's not difficult to make an impact on your world.
All you really have to do is put the needs of others
ahead of your own. You can make a difference
with a little time and a big heart.

James Dobson

— A Prayer —

Lord, make me a generous and cheerful giver.
Help me to give generously of my time and
my possessions as I care for those in need.
And, make me a humble giver, Lord,
so that all the glory and the praise might be Yours.

Amen

Gifts

As each one has received a gift, minister it to one another, as good stewards of the manifold grace of God.

1 Peter 4:10 NKJV

I remind you to fan into flame the gift of God.

2 Timothy 1:6 NIV

Now there are varieties of gifts, but the same Spirit. And there are varieties of ministries, and the same Lord.

1 Corinthians 12: 4, 5 NASB

"For I know the plans that I have for you," declares the Lord, "plans to prosper you and not to harm you, plans to give you hope and a future. Then you will call upon me and come and pray to me, and I will listen to you."

Jeremiah 29:11, 12 NLT

Every good gift and every perfect gift is from above and comes down from the Father of lights.

James 1:17 NKJV

All people have special gifts, and you are no exception. But, your gift is no guarantee of success; it must be cultivated and nurtured; otherwise, it will go unused . . . and God's gift to you will be squandered. Today, accept this challenge: value the talent that God has given you, nourish it, make it grow, and share it with the world. After all, the best way to say "Thank You" for God's gifts is to use them.

There's a unique sense of fulfillment that comes when we submit our gifts to God's use and ask him to energize them in a supernatural way—and then step back to watch what he does. It can be the difference between merely existing in black and white and living a life in full, brilliant color.

Lee Strobel

— A Prayer —

Dear Lord, let me use my gifts, and let me help my friends discover theirs. Your gifts are priceless and eternal. May we, Your children, use them to the glory of Your kingdom, today and forever.

Amen

God's Love

For the LORD your God has arrived to live among you.
He is a mighty savior. He will rejoice over you with
great gladness. With his love, he will calm all your fears.
He will exult over you by singing a happy song.

Zephaniah 3:17 NLT

His banner over me was love.

Song of Solomon 2:4 KJV

But the love of the Lord remains forever with those
who fear him. His salvation extends to the children's children
of those who are faithful to his covenant,
of those who obey his commandments!

Psalm 103:17, 18 NLT

For God so loved the world,
that he gave his only begotten Son,
that whosoever believeth in him should not perish,
but have everlasting life.

John 3:16 KJV

The Lord says, I will rescue those who love me.
I will protect those who trust in my name.

Psalm 91:14 NLT

God is love, and God's love is perfect. When we open our hearts to His perfect love, we are touched by the Creator's hand, and we are transformed, not just for a day, but for all eternity.

Today, as you carve out quiet moments of thanksgiving and praise for your Creator, open yourself to His presence and to His love.

Snuggle in God's arms. When you are hurting, when you feel lonely or left out, let Him cradle you, comfort you, reassure you of His all-sufficient power and love.

Kay Arthur

— *A Prayer* —

God, You are love. I love You, Lord,
and as I love You more, I am able to love
my family and friends more. Let me be
Your loving servant, Heavenly Father,
today and throughout eternity.

Amen

God's Mercy

He has shown you, O man, what is good;
And what does the LORD require of you but to do justly,
to love mercy, and to walk humbly with your God?

Micah 6:8 NKJV

And the LORD said, "I will cause all my goodness to pass in front of you, and I will proclaim my name, the LORD, in your presence. I will have mercy on whom I will have mercy, and I will have compassion on whom I will have compassion.

Exodus 33:19 NIV

But in your great mercy you did not put an end to them or abandon them, for you are a gracious and merciful God.

Nehemiah 9:31 NIV

The LORD is gracious and full of compassion,
Slow to anger and great in mercy.
The LORD is good to all,
And His tender mercies are over all His works.

Psalm 145:8, 9 NKJV

God offers us forgiveness and salvation. God's mercy, like His love, is infinite and everlasting—it knows no boundaries. As a demonstration of His mercy, God sent His only Son to die for our sins, and we must praise our Creator for that priceless gift.

As Christians, we have been blessed by a merciful, loving God. May we accept His mercy. And may we, in turn, show love and mercy to our friends, to our families, and to all whom He chooses to place along our paths.

God knows us inside out and outside in.
He understands what motivates us and accepts us
even in our worst moments.

Thelma Wells

— A Prayer —

Dear Lord, I have fallen short of Your commandments, and You have forgiven me. You have blessed me with Your love and Your mercy. Enable me to be merciful toward others, Father, just as You have been merciful to me, and let me share Your love with all whom I meet.

Amen

God's Plan

"I say this because I know what I am planning for you," says the Lord. "I have good plans for you, not plans to hurt you. I will give you hope and a good future."

Jeremiah 29:11 NCV

Now the God of peace . . . equip you in every good thing to do His will.

Hebrews 13:20, 21 NASB

Trust the Lord your God with all your heart and lean not on your own understanding; in all your ways acknowledge him, and he will make your paths straight.

Proverbs 3:5, 6 NIV

The Lord says, "I will guide you along the best pathway for your life. I will advise you and watch over you."

Psalm 32:8 NLT

The steps of a good man are ordered by the LORD . . . .

Psalm 37:23 KJV

God has a plan for your life. He understands that plan as thoroughly and completely as He knows you. And, if you seek God's will earnestly and prayerfully, He will make His plans known to you in His own time and in His own way.

Sometimes, God's plans seem unmistakably clear to you. But other times, He may lead you through the wilderness before He directs you to the Promised Land. So be patient and keep seeking His will for your life. When you do, you'll be amazed at the marvelous things that an all-powerful, all-knowing God can do.

Mark it down: things do not "just happen."
There is a God-arranged plan for this world of ours,
which includes a specific plan for you.

Charles Swindoll

— A Prayer —

Lord, You have a plan for my life. Let me discover it
and live it. Today, I will seek Your will,
knowing that when I trust in You, dear Father,
I am eternally blessed.

Amen

God's Support

Therefore humble yourselves under the mighty hand of God,
that He may exalt you at the proper time,
casting all your anxiety on Him, because He cares for you.

1 Peter 5:6, 7 NASB

And God is able to make all grace abound toward you,
that you, always having all sufficiency in all things,
may have an abundance for every good work.

2 Corinthians 9:8 NKJV

Finally, my brethren, be strong in the Lord and
in the power of His might. Put on the whole armor of God,
that you may be able to stand against the wiles of the devil.

Ephesians 6:10, 11 NKJV

The Lord is my shepherd; I shall not want.

Psalm 23:1 KJV

For the eyes of the Lord are toward the righteous,
and his ears attend to their prayers.

1 Peter 3:12 NASB

God is a never-ending source of support and courage for those of us who call upon Him. When we are weary, He gives us strength. When we see no hope, God reminds us of His promises. When we grieve, God wipes away our tears.

Do the demands of this day threaten to overwhelm you? If so, you must rely not only upon your own resources, but also upon the promises of your Father in heaven. God will hold your hand and walk with you every day of your life if you let Him. So even if your circumstances are difficult, trust the Father. His love is eternal and His goodness endures forever.

He stands fast as your rock, steadfast as your safeguard, sleepless as your watcher, valiant as your champion.

C. H. Spurgeon

— A Prayer —

Heavenly Father, You never leave or forsake me.
You are always with me, protecting me and
encouraging me. Whatever this day may bring,
I thank You for Your love and Your strength.
Let me lean upon You, Father, this day and forever.

Amen

God's Timing

Humble yourselves therefore under the mighty hand of God,
that he may exalt you in due time.

1 Peter 5:6 KJV

From one man he made every nation of men,
that they should inhabit the whole earth;
and he determined the times set for them
and the exact places where they should live.

Acts 17:26 NIV

He has made everything beautiful in its time.
He has also set eternity in the hearts of men; yet they cannot fathom what God has done from beginning to end.

Ecclesiastes 3:11 NIV

He said to them: "It is not for you to know the times
or dates the Father has set by his own authority."

Acts 1:7 NIV

The steps of the Godly are directed by the Lord.
He delights in every detail of their lives.
Though they stumble, they will not fall,
for the Lord holds them by the hand.

Psalm 37:23, 24 NLT

Are you anxious for God to work out His plan for your life? Who isn't? As believers, we all want God to do great things for us and through us, and we want Him to do those things now. But sometimes, God has other plans. Sometimes, God's timetable does not coincide with our own. It's worth noting, however, that God's timetable is always perfect.

God manages perfectly, day and night, year in and year out, the movements of the stars, the wheeling of the planets, the staggering coordination of events that goes on at the molecular level in order to hold things together. There is no doubt that He can manage the timing of my days and weeks.

Elisabeth Elliot

— A Prayer —

Lord, my sense of timing is fallible and imperfect;
Yours is not. Let me trust in Your timetable for my life,
and give me the patience and the wisdom
to trust Your plans, not my own.
Amen

God's Word

For the word of God is living and effective and sharper than any two-edged sword, penetrating as far as to divide soul, spirit, joints, and marrow; it is a judge of the ideas and thoughts of the heart.

Hebrews 4:12 HCSB

Heaven and earth will pass away, but my words will never pass away.

Matthew 24:35 NIV

Whosoever cometh to me, and heareth my sayings, and doeth them, I will show you to whom he is like: he is like a man which built a house, and digged deep, and laid the foundation on a rock: and when the flood arose, the stream beat vehemently upon that house, and could not shake it; for it was founded upon a rock.

Luke 6:47, 48 KJV

But he answered and said, It is written, Man shall not live by bread alone but by every word that proceedeth out of the mouth of God.

Matthew 4:4 KJV

The Bible is unlike any other book. A. W. Tozer wrote, "The purpose of the Bible is to bring men to Christ, to make them holy and prepare them for heaven. In this it is unique among books, and it always fulfills its purpose."

Jonathan Edwards advised, "Be assiduous in reading the Holy Scriptures. This is the fountain whence all knowledge in divinity must be derived. Therefore let not this treasure lie by you neglected." God's Holy Word is, indeed, a priceless, one-of-a-kind treasure. Handle it with care, but more importantly, handle it every day.

Weave the unveiling fabric of God's word through
your heart and mind. It will hold strong,
even if the rest of life unravels.

Gigi Graham Tchividjian

— A Prayer —

Heavenly Father, You have given me the gift of
Your Holy Word. Let me study it, and let me live
according to its principles. Let me read Your Word,
meditate upon it, and share its joyous message
with my friends, today and every day.

Amen

Golden Rule

See that no one renders evil for evil to anyone, but always pursue what is good both for yourselves and for all.

1 Thessalonians 5:15 NKJV

Bear ye one another's burdens, and so fulfil the law of Christ.

Galatians 6:2 KJV

This royal law is found in the Scriptures: "Love your neighbor as yourself." If you obey this law, then you are doing right.

James 2:8 ICB

I tell you the truth, whatever you did for one of the least of these brothers of mine, you did for me.

Matthew 25:40 NIV

Do to others as you would have them do to you.

Luke 6:31 NIV

The words of Luke 6:31 remind us that, as believers in Christ, we are commanded to treat others as we wish to be treated. This commandment is, indeed, the Golden Rule for Christians of every generation. When we weave the thread of kindness into the very fabric of our lives, we give glory to the One who gave His life for us.

The Golden Rule starts at home,
but it should never stop there.

Marie T. Freeman

— A Prayer —

Dear Lord, I thank You for friends and family members who practice the Golden Rule. Because I expect to be treated with kindness, let me be kind. Because I wish to be loved, let me be loving. Because I need forgiveness, let me be merciful. In all things, Lord, let me live by the Golden Rule, and let me express my gratitude to those who offer kindness and generosity to me.

Amen

Grace

And the God of all grace, who called you to his eternal glory in Christ, after you have suffered a little while, will himself restore you and make you strong, firm and steadfast.

1 Peter 5:10 NIV

My grace is sufficient for you,
for My strength is made perfect in weakness.

2 Corinthians 12:9 NKJV

In Him we have redemption through His blood,
the forgiveness of sins, according to the riches of His grace
which He made to abound toward us
in all wisdom and prudence . . . .

Ephesians 1:7, 8 KJV

But we see Jesus, who was made a little lower than the angels, now crowned with glory and honor because he suffered death, so that by the grace of God he might taste death for everyone.

Hebrews 2:9 NIV

For it is by grace you have been saved, through faith—
and this not from yourselves, it is the gift of God—
not by works, so that no one can boast.

Ephesians 2:8, 9 NIV

The familiar words of Ephesians 2:8 make God's promise perfectly clear: We are saved, not by our actions, but by God's mercy. We are saved, not because of our good deeds, but because of our faith in Christ.

God's grace is the ultimate gift, and we owe Him the ultimate in thanksgiving. Let us praise the Creator for His priceless gift, and let us share the Good News with all who cross our paths.

Costly grace is the treasure hidden in the field; for the sake of it, a man will gladly go and sell all that he has. It is costly because it costs a man his life, and it is grace because it gives a man the only true life.

Dietrich Bonhoeffer

— A Prayer —

Lord, You have saved me by Your grace.
Keep me mindful that Your grace is a gift that
I can accept but cannot earn. I praise You for that
priceless gift, today and forever. Let me share
the good news of Your grace with my friends
that need Your healing touch.

Amen

Gratitude

Everything created by God is good, and nothing is to be rejected, if it is received with gratitude; for it is sanctified by means of the word of God and prayer.

1 Timothy 4:4, 5 NASB

As you therefore have received Christ Jesus the Lord, so walk in Him, having been firmly rooted and now being built up in Him and established in your faith, just as you were instructed, and overflowing with gratitude.

Colossians 2:6, 7 NASB

Therefore, since we receive a kingdom which cannot be shaken, let us show gratitude by which we may offer to God an acceptable service with reverence and awe . . . .

Hebrews 12:28 NASB

In everything give thanks;
for this is God's will for you in Christ Jesus.

1 Thessalonians 5:18 NIV

And let the peace of God rule in your hearts . . .
and be ye thankful.

Colossians 3:15 KJV

For most of us, life is busy and complicated. We have countless responsibilities, some of which begin before sunrise and many of which end long after sunset. Amid the rush and crush of the daily grind, it is easy to lose sight of God and His blessings. But, when we forget to slow down and say "Thank You" to our Maker, we rob ourselves of His presence, His peace, and His joy.

Our task, as believing Christians, is to praise God many times each day. Then, with gratitude in our hearts, we can face our daily duties with the perspective and power that only He can provide.

A spirit of thankfulness makes all the difference.

Billy Graham

— A Prayer —

Dear Lord, You have given me much; when I think of Your grace and goodness, I am humbled and thankful. Today, I will praise You, not just through my words, but also through my deeds. Let the words that I speak and the actions that I take bring honor to You and to Your Son.

Amen

Grief

I have heard your prayer, I have seen your tears; behold, I will heal you.

2 Kings 20:5 NASB

You will be sad, but your sadness will become joy.

John 16:20 NCV

Blessed are those who mourn, because they will be comforted.

Matthew 5:4 HCSB

They that sow in tears shall reap in joy.

Psalm 126:5 KJV

I cried out to the Lord in my suffering, and he heard me. He set me free from all my fears.

Psalm 34:6 NLT

Grief is the price that life periodically exacts from those who live long and love deeply. When we lose a loved one, or when we experience any other profound loss, darkness overwhelms us for a while, and it seems as if we cannot summon the strength to face another day—but, with God's help, we can. During times of heartache, we can turn to God, first for solace and then for renewal. When we do, He comforts us and, in time, He heals us.

We cannot always understand the ways of
Almighty God—the crosses which he sends us,
the sacrifices which he demands of us. But, if we accept
with faith and resignation his holy will—
with no looking back to what might have been—
we are at peace.

Rose Fitzgerald Kennedy

— A Prayer —

Heavenly Father, Your Word promises that You will
not give us more than we can bear; You have promised
to lift us out of our grief and despair. Today, Lord,
I pray for those who mourn, and I thank You
for sustaining all of us in our days of sorrow.
May we trust You always and praise You forever.

Amen

Happiness

But the truly happy person is the one who carefully studies God's perfect law that makes people free. He continues to study it. He listens to God's teaching and does not forget what he heard. Then he obeys what God's teaching says. When he does this, it makes him happy.

James 1:25 ICB

Those who are pure in their thinking are happy,
because they will be with God.

Matthew 5:8 NCV

Happy are those who fear the Lord.
Yes, happy are those who delight in doing his commands.

Psalm 112:1 NLT

Happy is he . . . whose hope is in the Lord his God.

Psalm 146:5 KJV

Happy is the man that findeth wisdom,
and the man that getteth understanding.

Proverbs 3:13 KJV

Do you want to be happy? Here are some things you should do: Love God and His Son, Jesus; obey the Golden Rule; and always try to do the right thing. When you do these things, you'll discover that happiness goes hand-in-hand with good behavior.

The happiest people do not misbehave; the happiest people are not cruel or greedy. The happiest people don't say unkind things. The happiest people are those who love God and follow His rules—starting, of course, with the Golden one.

Christianity says we were created by a righteous God to flourish and be exhilarated in a righteous environment. God has "wired" us in such a way that the more righteous we are, the more we'll actually enjoy life.

Bill Hybels

— A Prayer —

Lord, make me a happy Christian. Let me rejoice in the gift of this day, and let me praise You for the gift of Your Son. Make me be a joyful teacher, Lord, as I share Your Good News with all those who need Your healing touch.

Amen

Honesty

Lead a quiet and peaceable life in all godliness and honesty.

1 Timothy 2:2 KJV

Good people will be guided by honesty.

Proverbs 11:3 ICB

Therefore, seeing we have this ministry, as we have received mercy, we faint not; but have renounced the hidden things of dishonesty, not walking in craftiness, nor handling the word of God deceitfully; but, by manifestation of the truth, commending ourselves to every man's conscience in the sight of God.

2 Corinthians 4:1, 2 KJV

Buy the truth and do not sell it;
get wisdom, discipline, and understanding.

Proverbs 23:23 NIV

. . . and ye shall know the truth,
and the truth shall make you free.

John 8:32 KJV

From the time we are children, we are taught that honesty is the best policy. But, honesty is not just the best policy, it is also God's policy. If we are to be servants worthy of His holy blessings, we must remember that truth is not just the best way, it is God's way.

The single most important element in any
human relationship is honesty—
with oneself, with God, and with others.

Catherine Marshall

— A Prayer —

Dear Lord, You command Your children to walk in truth. Let me be honest with my family and friends, and let me be honest with myself. Honesty isn't just the best policy, Lord; it's Your policy, and I will obey You by making it my policy, too.

Amen

Honoring God

Here is my final advice:
Honor God and obey his commands.

Ecclesiastes 12:13 ICB

Honor GOD with everything you own;
give him the first and the best. Your barns will burst,
your wine vats will brim over.

Proverbs 3:9, 10 MSG

Call upon Me in the day of trouble;
I shall rescue you, and you will honor Me.

Psalm 50:15 NASB

Surely the righteous shall give thanks unto thy name:
the upright shall dwell in thy presence.

Psalm 140:13 KJV

The LORD is my strength and song, and He has become
my salvation; He is my God, and I will praise Him . . . .

Exodus 15:2 NKJV

When we honor God and place Him at the center of our lives, every day is a cause for celebration. God fills each day to the brim with possibilities, and He challenges us to use our lives for His purposes.

Today is a non-renewable resource—once it's gone, it's gone forever. Our responsibility—as believers in a risen Christ—is to use this day in the service of God's will and in the service of His people.

We honor God by asking for great things when they are part of His promise. We dishonor Him and cheat ourselves when we ask for molehills where He has offered mountains.

Vance Havner

— A Prayer —

Heavenly Father, I honor You and praise You for the gift of Your Son Jesus. You have given me the priceless gift of eternal life. Make me Your faithful servant, and let me share the joyous news of Jesus Christ with a world that needs His healing touch this day and every day.

Amen

Hope

Let us hold on to the confession of our hope without wavering, for He who promised is faithful.

Hebrews 10:23 HCSB

This hope we have as an anchor of the soul,
a hope both sure and steadfast.

Hebrews 6:19 NASB

The Lord is good to those whose hope is in him,
to the one who seeks him;
it is good to wait quietly for the salvation of the Lord.

Lamentations 3:25-27 NIV

Be of good courage, and he shall strengthen your heart,
all ye that hope in the Lord.

Psalm 31:24 KJV

Happy is he who has the God of Jacob for his help,
whose hope is in the Lord his God.

Psalm 146:5 NKJV

The hope that the world offers is fleeting and imperfect. The hope that God offers is unchanging, unshakable, and unending. It is no wonder, then, that when we seek security from worldly sources, our hopes are often dashed. Thankfully, God has no such record of failure.

With God by your side, you need never lose hope. So today and every day, ask God for these things: clear perspective, mountain-moving faith, and the courage to do what needs doing. After all, no problem is too big for God—not even yours.

The hope we have in Jesus is the anchor for the soul—something sure and steadfast, preventing drifting or giving way, lowered to the depth of God's love.

Franklin Graham

— A Prayer —

Dear Lord, let my hopes always reside in You. If I become discouraged, let me turn to You. If I grow tired, let me find strength in You. You are my Father, and I will place my faith, my trust, and my hopes in You.

Amen

Integrity

Till I die, I will not deny my integrity.
I will maintain my righteousness and never let go of it;
my conscience will not reproach me as long as I live.

Job 27:5, 6 NIV

The integrity of the upright will guide them.

Proverbs 11:3 NKJV

The man of integrity walks securely,
but he who takes crooked paths will be found out.

Proverbs 10 9 NIV

In everything set them an example by doing what is good.
In your teaching show integrity, seriousness and
soundness of speech that cannot be condemned,
so that those who oppose you may be ashamed
because they have nothing bad to say about us.

Titus 2:7 NIV

Charles Swindoll correctly observed, "Nothing speaks louder or more powerfully than a life of integrity." Godly men and women agree. Integrity is built slowly over a lifetime. It is a precious thing—difficult to build but easy to tear down. As believers in Christ, we must seek to live each day with discipline, honesty, and faith. When we do, at least two things happen: integrity becomes a habit, and God blesses us because of our obedience to Him.

Living a life of integrity isn't always the easiest way, but it is always the right way. And God clearly intends that it should be our way, too.

Maintaining your integrity in a world of sham
is no small accomplishment.

Wayne Oates

— A Prayer —

Heavenly Father, Your Word instructs me to walk in
righteousness and with integrity. Make me
Your worthy servant, Lord. Let my words be true,
and let my actions influence my friends to trust You.
Amen

Jesus

Let us run with endurance the race that is set before us,
fixing our eyes on Jesus, the author and perfecter of faith,
who for the joy set before Him endured the cross,
despising the shame, and has sat down
at the right hand of the throne of God.

Hebrews 12:1, 2 NASB

Jesus Christ is the same yesterday and today and forever.

Hebrews 13:8 NASB

Jesus said to him, "I am the way, the truth, and the life.
No one comes to the Father except through Me.
If you had known Me, you would have known
My Father also; and from now on
you know Him and have seen Him."

John 14:6, 7 NKJV

God lifted him high and honored him far beyond anyone or anything, ever, so that all created beings in heaven and earth, even those long ago dead and buried, will bow in worship before this Jesus Christ, and call out in praise that he is the Master of all,
to the glorious honor of God the Father.

Philippians 2:9-11 MSG

The 19th-century writer Hannah Whitall Smith observed, "The crucial question for each of us is this: What do you think of Jesus, and do you yet have a personal acquaintance with Him?" Indeed, the answer to that question determines the quality, the course, and the direction of our lives today and for all eternity.

Let us love our Savior, praise Him, and share His message of salvation with our friends, with our neighbors, and with the world. When we do, we demonstrate that our acquaintance with the Master is not a passing fancy; it is, instead, the cornerstone and the touchstone of our lives.

Had Jesus been the Word become word, He would have
spun theories about life, but since he was
the Word become flesh, he put shoes on
all his theories and made them walk.

E. Stanley Jones

— A Prayer —

Dear Jesus, You are my Savior and my protector.
Give me the courage to trust You completely. Today,
I will praise You, I will honor You, and I will live
according to Your commandments, so that through me,
my friends might come to know Your perfect love.

Amen

Joy

Until now you have not asked for anything in my name. Ask and you will receive, so that your joy will be the fullest possible joy.

John 16:24 NCV

Always be full of joy in the Lord. I say it again—rejoice!

Philippians 4:4 NLT

These things have I spoken unto you, that my joy might remain in you, and that your joy might be full.

John 15:11 KJV

You will show me the way of life, granting me the joy of your presence and the pleasures of living with you forever.

Psalm 16:11 NLT

Rejoice, and be exceeding glad: for great is your reward in heaven . . . .

Matthew 5:12 KJV

Oswald Chambers correctly observed, "Joy is the great note all throughout the Bible." C. S. Lewis echoed that thought when he wrote, "Joy is the serious business of heaven." But, even the most dedicated Christians can, on occasion, forget to celebrate each day for what it is: a priceless gift from God.

Today, let us be joyful Christians with smiles on our faces and kind words on our lips. After all, this is God's day, and He has given us clear instructions for its use. We are commanded to rejoice and be glad. So, with no further ado, let the celebration begin.

Will you, with a glad and eager surrender, hand yourself and all that concerns you over into his hands? If you will do this, your soul will begin to know something of the joy of union with Christ.

Hannah Whitall Smith

— A Prayer —

Lord, make me a joyous Christian. Because of my salvation through Your Son, I have every reason to celebrate life. Let me share the joyful news of Jesus Christ to my friends, and let my life be a testimony to His love and to His grace.

Amen

Judging Others

*The Lord does not look at the things man looks at.
Man looks at the outward appearance,
but the Lord looks at the heart.*

1 Samuel 16:7 NIV

Speak and act as those who will be judged by the law of freedom. For judgment is without mercy to the one who hasn't shown mercy. Mercy triumphs over judgment.

James 2:12, 13 HCSB

*Judge not, and ye shall not be judged: condemn not,
and ye shall not be condemned: forgive,
and ye shall be forgiven . . . .*

Luke 6:37 KJV

*Either how canst thou say to thy brother, Brother, let me pull out the mote that is in thine eye, when thou thyself beholdest not the beam that is in thine own eye?
Thou hypocrite, cast out first the beam out of thine own eye, and then shalt thou see clearly to pull out the mote that is in thy brother's eye.*

Luke 6:42 KJV

Here's something worth thinking about: If you judge other people harshly, God will judge you in the same fashion. But that's not all (thank goodness!) The Bible also promises that if you forgive others, you, too, will be forgiven. Have you developed the bad habit of behaving yourself like an amateur judge and jury, assigning blame and condemnation wherever you go? If so, it's time to grow up and obey God. When it comes to judging everything and everybody, God doesn't need your help . . . and He doesn't want it.

Christians think they are prosecuting attorneys
or judges, when, in reality,
God has called all of us to be witnesses.

Warren Wiersbe

— *A Prayer* —

Lord, it's so easy to judge other people, but it's also easy to misjudge them. Only You can judge a human heart, Lord, so let me love my friends and neighbors, and let me help them, but never let me judge them.

Amen

Kindness

This is what the LORD *Almighty says:*
Judge fairly and honestly,
and show mercy and kindness to one another.

Zechariah 7:9 NLT

Be peaceable, gentle, showing every consideration
for all men.

Titus 3:2 NASB

Be kindly affectionate to one another with brotherly love,
in honor giving preference to one another;
not lagging in diligence, fervent in spirit,
serving the Lord; rejoicing in hope, patient in tribulation,
continuing steadfastly in prayer.

Romans 12:10-12 NKJV

A kind man benefits himself,
but a cruel man brings trouble on himself.

Proverbs 11:17 NIV

A new commandment I give unto you,
That ye love one another; as I have loved you . . . .

John 13:34 KJV

In the busyness and confusion of daily life, it is easy to lose focus, and it is easy to become frustrated. We are imperfect human beings struggling to manage our lives as best we can, but we often fall short. When we are distracted or disappointed, we may neglect to share a kind word or a kind deed. This oversight hurts others, but it hurts us most of all.

Today, slow yourself down and be alert for those who need your smile, your kind words, or your helping hand. Make kindness a centerpiece of your dealings with others. They will be blessed, and you will be, too.

When you launch an act of kindness out into
the crosswinds of life, it will blow kindness back to you.

Dennis Swanberg

— A Prayer —

Heavenly Father, thank You for the kindness of friends.
You have brought loving friends and family members
into my life. Let me return their kindness and
their love. I praise You, Father, for the dear people
who have enriched my life; may I, in turn, enrich theirs.

Amen

Knowledge

The knowledge of the secrets of the kingdom of heaven has been given to you . . . .

Matthew 13:11 NIV

For this very reason, make every effort to supplement your faith with goodness, goodness with knowledge, knowledge with self-control, self-control with endurance, endurance with godliness.

2 Peter 1:5, 6 HCSB

The fear of the Lord is the beginning of knowledge, but fools despise wisdom and discipline.

Proverbs 1:7 NIV

For the Lord giveth wisdom: out of his mouth cometh knowledge and understanding.

Proverbs 2:6 KJV

Reverence for the Lord is the foundation of true wisdom. The rewards of wisdom come to all who obey him.

Psalm 111:10 NLT

If we are to grow as Christians, we need both knowledge and wisdom. Knowledge is found in textbooks. Wisdom, on the other hand, is found in God's Holy Word and in the carefully-chosen words of loving parents, family members, and friends. Knowledge is an important building block in a well-lived life, and it pays rich dividends both personally and professionally. But, wisdom is even more important because it refashions not only the mind, but also the heart.

It's the things you learn after you know it all
that really count.

Vance Havner

— A Prayer —

Lord, You are my Teacher. Help me to be a student of Your Word and a servant of Your will. Let me live by the truth You reveal, let me trust in the wisdom of Your commandments, and let me teach my friends the glory of Your ways.

Amen

Laughter

Shout joyfully to the Lord, all the earth; Break forth in song, rejoice, and sing praises. Sing to the Lord with the harp,
With the harp and the sound of a psalm,
With trumpets and the sound of a horn;
Shout joyfully before the Lord, the King.

Psalm 98:4-6 NIV

A happy heart is like good medicine.

Proverbs 17:22 NCV

There is a time for everything, and a season for every activity under heaven . . . a time to weep and a time to laugh, a time to mourn and a time to dance.

Ecclesiastes 3:1, 4 NIV

Oh, clap your hands, all you peoples!
Shout to God with the voice of triumph!

Psalm 47:1 NKJV

This is the day which the Lord hath made;
we will rejoice and be glad in it.

Psalm 118:24 KJV

Laughter is God's gift, and He intends that we enjoy it. Yet sometimes, because of the inevitable stresses of everyday life, laughter seems only a distant memory. As Christians we have every reason to be cheerful and to be thankful. Our blessings from God are beyond measure, starting, of course, with a gift that is ours for the asking, God's gift of salvation through Christ Jesus.

Today, as you go about your daily activities, approach life with a smile and a chuckle. After all, God created laughter for a reason . . . and Father indeed knows best. So laugh!

There is nothing that rejuvenates the parched,
delicate spirits of children faster than when
a lighthearted spirit pervades the home
and laughter fills its halls.

James Dobson

— A Prayer —

Dear Lord, laughter is Your gift to me; help me to enjoy
it. Today and every day, put a smile on my face,
and help me to share that smile with my family
and friends. This is the day that You have made, Lord.
Let me enjoy it . . . and let me laugh.

Amen

Loving God

And we know that in all things God works for the good of those who love him, who have been called according to his purpose.

Romans 8:28 NIV

Jesus replied, "'Love the Lord your God with all your heart and with all your soul and with all your mind.' This is the first and greatest commandment. And the second is like it: 'Love your neighbor as yourself.' All the Law and the Prophets hang on these two commandments."

Matthew 22:37-40 NIV

For this is the love of God,
that we keep his commandments . . . .

1 John 5:3 KJV

I will thank you, Lord with all my heart;
I will tell of all the marvelous things you have done.
I will be filled with joy because of you.
I will sing praises to your name, O Most High.

Psalm 9:1, 2 NLT

When we worship God with faith and assurance, when we place Him at the absolute center of our lives, we invite His love into our hearts. In turn, we grow to love Him more deeply as we sense His love for us. St. Augustine wrote, "I love you, Lord, not doubtingly, but with absolute certainty. Your Word beat upon my heart until I fell in love with you, and now the universe and everything in it tells me to love you." Let us pray that we, too, will turn our hearts to our Father, knowing with certainty that He loves us and that we love Him.

When we develop an authentic love relationship
with God, we will not be able to keep Him
compartmentalized in "churchy," religious categories.

Beth Moore

— A Prayer —

Dear Heavenly Father, You have blessed me with
a love that is infinite and eternal. Let me love You,
Lord, more and more each day. Make me a loving
servant, Father, today and throughout eternity.
And, let me show my love for You by sharing
Your message and Your love with others.

Amen

Loving Others

*A new command I give you: Love one another.
As I have loved you, so you must love one another.
By this all men will know you are my disciples,
if you love one another.*

John 13:34, 35 NIV

*Let's see how inventive we can be in encouraging love
and helping out, not avoiding worshipping
together as some do but spurring each other on.*

Hebrews 10:24, 25 MSG

*And this commandment have we from him,
That he who loveth God love his brother also.*

1 John 4:21 KJV

*And the Lord make you to increase and abound
in love one toward another, and toward all men . . . .*

1 Thessalonians 3:12 KJV

*But now faith, hope, love, abide these three;
but the greatest of these is love.*

1 Corinthians 13:13 NASB

The words of 1st Corinthians 13 remind us that faith is important, and so, too, is hope. But love is more important still. Christ showed His love for us on the cross, and, as Christians, we are called upon to return Christ's love by sharing it. Today, let us spread Christ's love by word and by example. And the greatest of these, of course, is example.

We have the Lord, but He Himself has recognized
that we need the touch of a human hand.
He Himself came down and lived among us as a man.
We cannot see Him now, but blessed be the tie that
binds human hearts in Christian love.

Vance Havner

— A Prayer —

Heavenly Father, You have given me love that is beyond human understanding, and I am Your loving servant. May the love that I feel for You be reflected in the compassion that I show toward my family and friends. Let me show compassion and understanding to those who cross my path this day and every day.

Amen

Miracles

But as it is written: "Eye has not seen, nor ear heard, nor have entered into the heart of man the things which God has prepared for those who love Him."

1 Corinthians 2:9 NKJV

God verified the message by signs and wonders and various miracles and by giving gifts of the Holy Spirit whenever he chose to do so.

Hebrews 2:4 NLT

But Jesus looked at them and said to them,
"With men this is impossible,
but with God all things are possible."

Matthew 19:26 NKJV

Search for the Lord and for his strength,
and keep on searching.
Think of the wonderful works he has done,
the miracles and the judgements he handed down.

Psalm 105: 4, 5 NLT

Is anything too hard for the Lord?

Genesis 18:14 KJV

Do you believe in God's miraculous provision? You should. But perhaps, as you have faced the inevitable struggles of life, you have, without realizing it, placed limitations on God. To do so is a profound mistake. God's power has no limitations. God can work mighty miracles in your own life if you let Him.

Are you a "Doubting Thomas," or a "Negative Nancy"? If so, you are attempting to place limitations on a God who has none. Instead, you must trust in God. Instead of doubting His power, trust it. When you do, He will change your life now and throughout eternity.

Too many Christians live below the miracle level.

Vance Havner

— A Prayer —

Dear Lord, absolutely nothing is impossible for You. Let me trust in Your power and in Your miracles. When I lose hope, give me faith; when others lose hope, let me tell them of Your glorious works. Today, Lord, keep me mindful that You are a God of infinite possibilities and infinite love.

Amen

New Beginnings

I will give you a new heart and put a new spirit in you . . . .

Ezekiel 36:26 NIV

The Lord says, "Forget what happened before,
and do not think about the past. Look at the new thing
I am going to do. It is already happening. Don't you see it?
I will make a road in the desert and rivers in the dry land."

Isaiah 43:18, 19 NCV

Create in me a clean heart, O God;
and renew a right spirit within me.

Psalm 51:10 KJV

And He who sits on the throne said,
"Behold, I am making all things new."

Revelation 21:5 NASB

But those who wait on the Lord Shall renew their strength;
They shall mount up with wings like eagles,
They shall run and not be weary,
They shall walk and not faint.

Isaiah 40:31 NKJV

Today, like every other day, is literally brimming with possibilities. Whether we realize it or not, God is always working in us and through us; our job is to let Him do His work without undo interference. Yet we are imperfect beings who, because of our limited vision, often resist God's will. We want life to unfold according to our own desires, not God's. But, our Heavenly Father may have other plans.

Today, think carefully about the work that God can do through you. And then, set out upon the next phase of your life's journey with a renewed sense of purpose and hope. God has the power to make all things new, including you. Your job is to let Him do it.

No matter how badly we have failed,
we can always get up and begin again.
Our God is the God of new beginnings.

Warren Wiersbe

— A Prayer —

O Lord, my Creator, conform me to Your image.
Create in me a clean heart, a new heart, that reflects
the love You lavish on me. Where I need to change,
change me, and make me new.

Amen

Obedience

*And being found in appearance as a man,
he humbled himself and became obedient to death—
even death on a cross!*

Philippians 2:8 NIV

*Therefore whoever hears these sayings of Mine,
and does them, I will liken him to a wise man who built his
house on the rock: and the rain descended, the floods came,
and the winds blew and beat on that house;
and it did not fall, for it was founded on the rock.*

Matthew 7:24, 25 NKJV

*Then he went down to Nazareth with them and was obedient
to them. But his mother treasured all these things in
her heart. And Jesus grew in wisdom and stature,
and in favor with God and men.*

Luke 2:51 NIV

*Jesus answered and said unto him, If a man love me,
he will keep my words: and my Father will love him,
and we will come unto him, and make our abode with him.*

John 14:23 KJV

God's commandments are not "suggestions," and they are not "helpful hints." They are, instead, immutable laws which, if followed, lead to repentance, salvation, and abundance. But if you choose to disobey the commandments of your Heavenly Father or the teachings of His Son, you will most surely reap a harvest of regret.

The formula for a successful life is surprisingly straightforward: Study God's Word and obey it. Does this sound too simple? Perhaps it is simple, but it is also the only way to reap the marvelous riches that God has in store for You.

Obedience invites Christ to show his incomparable strength in our mortal weakness.

Beth Moore

— A Prayer —

Dear Lord, when I am tempted to disobey Your commandments, correct my errors and guide my path. Make me a faithful steward of my talents, my opportunities, and my possessions so that Your Kingdom may be glorified, now and forever.

Amen

Optimism

But if we look forward to something we don't have yet,
we must wait patiently and confidently.

Romans 8:25 NLT

For God has not given us a spirit of fear,
but of power and of love and of a sound mind.

2 Timothy 1:7 NLT

These things have I spoken unto you,
that my joy might remain in you,
and that your joy might be full.

John 15:11 KJV

Finally, brethren, whatsoever things are true,
whatsoever things are honest, whatsoever things are just,
whatsoever things are pure, whatsoever things are lovely,
whatsoever things are of good report; if there be any virtue,
and if there be any praise, think on these things.

Philippians 4:8 KJV

Are you an optimistic, hopeful, enthusiastic Christian? You should be. After all, as a believer, you have every reason to be optimistic about life here on earth and life eternal. As C. H. Spurgeon observed, "Our hope in Christ for the future is the mainstream of our joy." But sometimes, you may find yourself pulled down by the inevitable demands and worries of life here on earth. If you find yourself discouraged, exhausted, or both, then it's time to take your concerns to God. When you do, He will lift your spirits and renew your strength.

Go forward confidently, energetically
attacking problems, expecting favorable outcomes.

Norman Vincent Peale

— *A Prayer* —

Dear Lord, You love me, You care for me, and
You protect me. Because of You, Father, and because
of Your Son, I can live each day with celebration in my
heart and praise on my lips. Let me always be thankful,
and let me share the Good News of Jesus as I turn
my thoughts to You this day and always.

Amen

Peace

And the peace of God, which surpasses all understanding,
will guard your hearts and minds through Christ Jesus.
Finally, brethren, whatever things are true,
whatever things are noble, whatever things are just,
whatever things are pure, whatever things are lovely,
whatever things are of good report, if there is any virtue
and if there is anything praiseworthy—
meditate on these things.

Philippians 4:7, 8 NKJV

And let the peace of God rule in your hearts . . .
and be ye thankful.

Colossians 3:15 KJV

Be perfect, be of good comfort, be of one mind, live in peace;
and the God of love and peace shall be with you.

2 Corinthians 13:11 KJV

Peace I leave with you, my peace I give unto you:
not as the world giveth, give I unto you.
Let not your heart be troubled, neither let it be afraid.

John 14:27 KJV

Have you found the genuine peace that can be yours through Jesus Christ? Or are you still rushing after the illusion of "peace and happiness" that the world promises but cannot deliver?

Today, as a gift to yourself, to your family, and to the world, let Christ's peace become your peace. Let Him rule your heart and your thoughts. When you do, you will partake in the peace that only He can give.

O God, Thou hast made us for Thyself,
and our hearts are restless
until they find their rest in Thee.

St. Augustine

— A Prayer —

The world talks about peace, but only You, Lord, can give a perfect and lasting peace. True peace comes through the Prince of Peace, and sometimes His peace passes all understanding. Help me to accept His peace—and share it with my friends—this day and forever.

Amen

Perseverance

Indeed we count them blessed who endure.

James 5:11 NKJV

Don't look for shortcuts to God. The market is flooded with surefire, easygoing formulas for a successful life that can be practiced in your spare time. Don't fall for that stuff, even though crowds of people do. The way to life—to God!—is vigorous and requires total attention.

Matthew 7:13, 14 MSG

Let us run with endurance the race that is set before us, fixing our eyes on Jesus, the author and perfecter of faith.

Hebrews 12:1, 2 NASB

I do not consider myself yet to have taken hold of it. But one thing I do: Forgetting what is behind and straining toward what is ahead, I press on toward the goal to win the prize for which God has called me heavenward in Christ Jesus.

Philippians 3:13, 14 NIV

We must not become tired of doing good.

Galatians 6:2 ICB

In a world filled with roadblocks and stumbling blocks, we need strength, courage, and perseverance. And, as an example of perfect perseverance, we need look no further than our Savior, Jesus Christ.

Jesus finished what He began. Despite the torture He endured, despite the shame of the cross, Jesus was steadfast in His faithfulness to God. We, too, must remain faithful, especially during times of hardship.

I learned as never before that persistent calling upon the Lord breaks through every stronghold of the devil, for nothing is impossible with God. For Christians in these troubled times, there is simply no other way.

Jim Cymbala

— A Prayer —

Lord, when life is difficult, I am tempted to abandon hope in the future. But You are my God, and I can draw strength from You. Let me trust You, Father, in good times and in bad times. Let me persevere—even if my soul is troubled—and let me follow Your Son Jesus Christ this day and forever.

Amen

Politeness

*Are there those among you who are truly wise
and understanding? Then they should show it by living right
and doing good things with a gentleness
that comes from wisdom.*

James 3:13 NCV

*A good person produces good deeds from a good heart,
and an evil person produces evil deeds from an evil heart.
Whatever is in your heart determines what you say.*

Luke 6:45 NLT

Use hospitality one to another without grudging.

1 Peter 4:9 KJV

Be gentle unto all men, apt to teach, patient.

2 Timothy 2:24 KJV

*And be ye kind one to another, tenderhearted,
forgiving one another,
even as God for Christ's sake hath forgiven you.*

Ephesians 4:32 KJV

Did Christ instruct us in matters of etiquette and courtesy? Of course He did. Christ's instructions are clear: "In everything, therefore, treat people the same way you want them to treat you, for this is the Law and the Prophets" (Matthew 7:12 NASB). Jesus did not say, "In some things, treat people as you wish to be treated." And, He did not say, "From time to time, treat others with kindness." Christ said that we should treat others as we wish to be treated in every aspect of our daily lives. This, of course, is a tall order indeed, but as Christians, we are commanded to do our best.

As you consider all the things that Christ has done in your life, honor Him with your words and with your deeds. He expects no less, and He deserves no less.

Courtesy is contagious.

Marie T. Freeman

— A Prayer —

Guide me this day, O Lord, to treat all those I meet with courtesy and respect. You have created each person in Your own image; let me honor those who cross my path with the dignity that You have bestowed upon them. We are all Your children, Lord; let me show kindness to Your children.

Amen

Praise

Sing to the Lord, all the earth; Proclaim the good news of His salvation from day to day.

1 Chronicles 16:23 NKJV

Through Him then, let us continually offer up a sacrifice of praise to God, that is, the fruit of lips that give thanks to His name.

Hebrews 13:15 NASB

Praise ye the LORD. O give thanks unto the LORD; for he is good: for his mercy endureth forever.

Psalm 106:1 KJV

Rejoice evermore. Pray without ceasing. In every thing give thanks: for this is the will of God in Christ Jesus concerning you.

1 Thessalonians 5:16-18 KJV

It is good to give thanks to the Lord, to sing praises to the Most High. It is good to proclaim your unfailing love in the morning, your faithfulness in the evening.

Psalm 92:2, 3 NLT

The Bible makes it clear: it pays to praise God. But sometimes, we allow ourselves to become so preoccupied with the demands of everyday life that we forget to say "Thank You" to the Giver of all good gifts.

Do you sincerely desire to be a worthy servant of the One who has given you eternal love and eternal life? Then praise Him for who He is and for what He has done for you. And don't just praise Him on Sunday morning. Praise Him all day long, every day, for as long as you live . . . and then for all eternity.

Our God is the sovereign Creator of the universe!
He loves us as His own children and
has provided every good thing we have;
He is worthy of our praise every moment.

Shirley Dobson

— A Prayer —

Heavenly Father, I come to You today with hope in my heart and praise on my lips. Make me a faithful steward of the blessings You have entrusted to me. Let me follow in Christ's footsteps today and every day that I live. And let my words and deeds praise You now and forever.

Amen

Pride

But God has chosen the foolish things of the world to put to shame the wise, and God has chosen the weak things of the world to put to shame the things which are mighty.

1 Corinthians 1:27 NKJV

. . . and all of you, clothe yourselves with humility toward one another, for God is opposed to the proud, but gives grace to the humble.

1 Peter 5:5 NASB

Those who walk in pride he [God] is able to humble.

Daniel 4:37 NIV

God opposes the proud but gives grace to the humble.

James 4:6 NIV

I will boast only in the Lord . . . .

Psalm 34:2 NLT

Sometimes our faith is tested more by prosperity than by adversity. Why? Because in times of plenty, we are tempted to stick out our chests and say, "I did that." But nothing could be further from the truth. All of our blessings start and end with God, and whatever "it" is, He did it. And He deserves the credit.

Who are the greatest among us? Are they the proud and the powerful? Hardly. The greatest among us are the humble servants who care less for their own glory and more for God's glory. If we seek greatness in God's eyes, we must forever praise God's good works, not our own.

God gives grace to the humble, not to the prideful.
If we assume self-advancing attitudes,
we've missed His gift of favor.

Franklin Graham

— A Prayer —

Heavenly Father, Jesus clothed Himself with humility
when He chose to leave heaven and come to earth
to live and die for all creation. Christ is my Master
and my example. Clothe me with humility, Lord,
so that I might be more like Your Son.

Amen

Quiet Time

In quietness and trust is your strength.

Isaiah 30:15 NASB

Be still, and know that I am God.

Psalm 46:10 NKJV

I wait quietly before God, for my hope is in him.

Psalm 62:5 NLT

And he withdrew himself into the wilderness, and prayed.

Luke 5:16 KJV

The effective prayer of a righteous man can accomplish much.

James 5:16 NASB

Are you one of those busy people who rush through the day with scarcely a single moment for quiet contemplation and prayer? If so, it's time to reorder your priorities.

Has the busy pace of life robbed you of the peace that might otherwise be yours through Jesus Christ? Nothing is more important than the time you spend with your Savior. So be still and claim the inner peace that is your spiritual birthright: the peace of Jesus Christ. It is offered freely; it has been paid for in full; it is yours for the asking. So ask. And then share.

In the center of a hurricane there is absolute
quiet and peace. There is no safer place
than in the center of the will of God.

Corrie ten Boom

— A Prayer —

Lord, Your Holy Word is a light unto the world;
let me study it, trust it, and share it with all my friends.
Let me discover You, Father, in the quiet moments of
the day. And, in all that I say and do, help me to be
a worthy witness as I share the Good News of
Your perfect Son and Your perfect Word.

Amen

Repentance

If My people who are called by My name will humble themselves, and pray and seek My face, and turn from their wicked ways, then I will hear from heaven, and will forgive their sin and heal their land.

2 Chronicles 7:14 NKJV

I preached that they should repent and turn to God and prove their repentance by their deeds.

Acts 26:20 NIV

Therefore this is what the Lord says: "If you repent, I will restore you that you may serve me . . . ."

Jeremiah 15:19 NIV

But their scribes and Pharisees murmured against his disciples, saying, Why do ye eat and drink with publicans and sinners? And Jesus answering said unto them, They that are whole need not a physician; but they that are sick. I came not to call the righteous, but sinners to repentance.

Luke 5:30-32 KJV

Genuine repentance requires more than simply offering God apologies for our misdeeds. Real repentance may start with feelings of sorrow and remorse, but it ends only when we turn away from the sin that has heretofore distanced us from our Creator. In truth, we offer our most meaningful apologies to God, not with our words, but with our actions.

Is there an aspect of your life that is distancing you from your God? If so, ask for His forgiveness, and—just as importantly—stop sinning. Then, wrap yourself in the protection of God's Word. When you do, you will be secure.

Repentance was perhaps best defined by a small girl:
It's to be sorry enough to quit.

C. H. Kilmer

— A Prayer —

When I stray from Your commandments, Lord, I must not only confess my sins, I must also turn from them. When I fall short, help me to change. When I reject Your Word and Your will for my life, guide me back to Your side. Forgive my sins, Dear Lord, and help me live according to Your plan for my life. Your plan is perfect, Father; I am not. Let me trust in You.

Amen

Righteousness

For the eyes of the Lord are on the righteous,
and His ears are open to their prayers;
but the face of the Lord is against those who do evil.

1 Peter 3:12 NKJV

The LORD has sought out for Himself a man
after His own heart.

1 Samuel 13:14 NASB

Walk in a manner worthy of the God who calls you
into His own kingdom and glory.

1 Thessalonians 2:12 NASB

Blessed are those whose way is blameless,
who walk in the law of the Lord. Blessed are those who keep
his testimonies, who seek him with their whole heart.

Psalm 119:1, 2 RSV

For thou, LORD, wilt bless the righteous . . . .

Psalm 5:12 KJV

How do we live a life that is "right with God?" By accepting God's Son and obeying His commandments. Accepting Christ is a decision that we make one time; following in His footsteps requires thousands of decisions each day.

Whose steps will you follow today? Will you honor God as you strive to follow His Son? Or will you join the lockstep legion that seeks to discover happiness and fulfillment through worldly means? If you are righteous and wise, you will follow Christ. You will follow Him today and every day. When you do so, you will be "right with God" precisely because you are walking aright with His only begotten Son.

The soul of a righteous person is nothing but a paradise, in which, as God tells us, he takes his delight.

St. Teresa of Avila

— *A Prayer* —

Lord, Your laws are perfect; let me live by those laws. And, let my life be a testimony to the power of righteousness and to the wisdom of Your commandments.

Amen

Satisfaction

*Satisfy us in the morning with your unfailing love,
that we may sing for joy and be glad all our days.*

Psalm 90:14 NIV

The righteous eat to their hearts' content . . . .

Proverbs 13:25 NIV

*I know what it is to be in need, and I know what it is to have plenty. I have learned the secret of being content in any and every situation, whether well fed or hungry, whether living in plenty or in want.
I can do everything through him who gives me strength.*

Philippians 4:12, 13 NIV

Let your character be free from the love of money, being content with what you have; for He Himself has said, "I will never desert you, nor will I ever forsake you."

Hebrews 13:5 NASB

Serving God does make us very rich, if we are satisfied with what we have. We brought nothing into the world, so we can take nothing out. But, if we have food and clothes, we will be satisfied with that.

1 Timothy 6:6-8 NCV

Where can we find satisfaction? Is it a result of wealth, or power, or fame? Hardly. Genuine contentment is a gift from God to those who trust in Him and follow His commandments. When God dwells at the center of our lives, contentment will belong to us just as surely as we belong to God.

To a world that was spiritually dry and populated
with parched lives scorched by sin,
Jesus was the Living Water who would quench
the thirsty soul, saving it from "bondage" and
filling it with satisfaction and joy and
purpose and meaning.

Anne Graham Lotz

— A Prayer —

Father, show me how to be ambitious in Your work.
Let me strive to do Your will here on earth, and as I do,
let me find contentment and balance. Let me live in the
light of Your will and Your priorities for my life,
and when I have done my best, Lord, give me
the wisdom to place my faith and my trust in You.

Amen

Serving God

Be strong and of good courage, and do it; do not fear nor be dismayed, for the Lord God—my God—will be with you. He will not leave you nor forsake you, until you have finished all the work for the service of the house of the Lord.

1 Chronicles 28:20 NKJV

No servant can serve two masters. Either he will hate the one and love the other, or he will be devoted to the one and despise the other. You cannot serve both God and Money.

Luke 16:13 NIV

Well done, good and faithful servant; you were faithful over a few things, I will make you ruler over many things. Enter into the joy of your lord.

Matthew 25:21 NKJV

Store up for yourselves treasures in heaven, where moth and rust do not destroy, and where thieves do not break in and steal. For where your treasure is there your heart will be also.

Matthew 6:20, 21 NIV

Are you excited about serving God? You should be. As a believer living in today's challenging world, you have countless opportunities to honor your Father in Heaven by serving Him.

Far too many Christians seem bored with their faith and stressed by their service. Don't allow yourself to become one of them! Serve God with thanksgiving in your heart and praise on your lips. Make your service to Him a time of celebration and thanksgiving. Worship your Creator by working for Him, joyfully, faithfully, and often.

There is nothing small in the service of God.

St. Francis of Sales

— A Prayer —

Lord, I can serve only one master; let me serve You. Let my actions be pleasing to You; let my words reflect Your infinite love; let my prayers be sincere and my thoughts be pure. In everything that I do, Father, let me praise You and serve You today and for eternity.

Amen

Serving Others

Suppose a brother or a sister is without clothes and daily food. If one of you says to him, "Go, I wish you well; keep warm and well fed," but does nothing about his physical needs, what good is it?

James 2:15, 16 NIV

And he sat down, and called the twelve, and saith unto them, If any man desire to be first, the same shall be last of all, and servant of all.

Mark 9:35 KJV

Even so faith, if it hath not works, is dead, being alone.

James 2:17 KJV

Therefore, since we receive a kingdom which cannot be shaken, let us show gratitude by which we may offer to God an acceptable service with reverence and awe.

Hebrews 12:28 NASB

We live in a world that glorifies power, prestige, fame, and money. But the words of Jesus teach us that the most esteemed men and women in this world are not the powerful or the wealthy. In God's eyes, the greatest of all are the servants of all.

Today, you may feel the temptation to build yourself up in the eyes of your neighbors. Resist that temptation. Instead, serve your neighbors quietly and without fanfare. Find a need and fill it . . . humbly. Lend a helping hand and share a word of kindness . . . anonymously. This is God's way.

I have discovered that when I please Christ,
I end up inadvertently serving others
far more effectively.

Beth Moore

— A Prayer —

Dear Lord, give me a servant's heart.
When Jesus humbled Himself and became a servant,
He also became an example for His followers.
Make me a faithful steward of my gifts,
and let me share with those in need.

Amen

Sharing

If you have two coats, give one to the poor.
If you have food, share it with those who are hungry.

Luke 3:11 NLT

In everything I did, I showed you that by this kind of hard work we must help the weak,
remembering the words the Lord Jesus himself said:
"It is more blessed to give than to receive."

Acts 20:35 NIV

. . . the righteous give without sparing.

Proverbs 21:26 NIV

You are the light of the world. A city on a hill cannot be hidden. Neither do people light a lamp and put it under a bowl. Instead they put it on its stand, and it gives light to everyone in the house. In the same way, let your light shine before men, that they may see your good deeds and praise your Father in heaven.

Matthew 5:14, 16 NIV

Sometimes, amid the busyness and distractions of this complicated world, we may fail to share our possessions, our talents, or our time. Yet, God commands that we treat others as we wish to be treated. God's Word makes it clear: We must be generous with others just as we seek generosity for ourselves.

As believers in Christ, we are blessed here on earth, and we are blessed eternally through God's grace. We can never fully repay God for His gifts, but we can share them with others. When we give sacrificially, our blessings are multiplied . . . and so is our joy.

It's a joy to share my faith. I've found something so special that I want others to share in it.

When something is that close to your heart, share it.

Michael Chang

— A Prayer —

Lord, there can be no delight in keeping
Your blessings for myself. True joy is found in sharing
what I have with friends and family. Make me
a generous, loving, humble person, Dear Lord,
as I follow the example of Your Son.

Amen

Sin

If we say that we have no sin, we deceive ourselves, and the truth is not in us. If we confess our sins, He is faithful and just to forgive us our sins and to cleanse us from all unrighteousness.

1 John 1:8, 9 NKJV

Therefore, since Christ suffered in his body, arm yourselves also with the same attitude, because he who has suffered in his body is done with sin. As a result, he does not live the rest of his earthly life for evil human desires, but rather for the will of God.

1 Peter 4:1, 2 NIV

Create in me a clean heart, O God; and renew a right spirit within me.

Psalm 51:10 KJV

But now being made free from sin, and become servants to God, ye have your fruit unto holiness, and the end everlasting life. For the wages of sin is death; but the gift of God is eternal life through Jesus Christ our Lord.

Romans 6:22, 23 KJV

As creatures of free will, we may disobey God whenever we choose, but when we do so, we put ourselves and our loved ones in peril. Why? Because disobedience invites disaster. We cannot sin against God without consequence. We cannot live outside His will without injury. Sins of all shapes and sizes have the power to do us great harm. And in a world where sin is big business, that's certainly a sobering thought.

An exalted view of God brings a clear view of sin
and a realistic view of self.

Henry Blackaby

— *A Prayer* —

Dear Lord, I am an imperfect human being.
When I have sinned, let me repent from my
wrongdoings, and let me seek forgiveness—
first from You, then from others,
and finally from myself.
Amen

Speech

So then, rid yourselves of all evil, all lying, hypocrisy, jealousy, and evil speech. As newborn babies want milk, you should want the pure and simple teaching. By it you can grow up and be saved.

1 Peter 2:1, 2 NCV

Watch the way you talk. Let nothing foul or dirty come out of your mouth. Say only what helps, each word a gift.

Ephesians 4:29 MSG

A word aptly spoken is like apples of gold in settings of silver.

Proverbs 25:11 NIV

May the words of my mouth and the meditation of my heart
be pleasing in your sight, O LORD,
my Rock and my Redeemer.

Psalm 19:14 NIV

Do you seek to be a source of encouragement to others? And, do you seek to be a worthy ambassador for Christ? If so, you must speak words that are worthy of your Savior. Avoid angry outbursts. Refrain from impulsive outpourings. Terminate tantrums. Instead, speak words of encouragement and hope to a world that desperately needs both.

Change the heart, and you change the speech.

Warren Wiersbe

— A Prayer —

Dear Lord, make my words pleasing to You.
Let me be a source of encouragement to my friends
and family as I share a message of faith and assurance
with the world. Today, I will honor You, Father,
by choosing my words carefully,
thoughtfully, and lovingly.
Amen

Spiritual Growth

*Long for the pure milk of the word,
so that by it you may grow in respect to salvation.*
1 Peter 2:2 NASB

*For this reason we also, since the day we heard it,
do not cease to pray for you, and to ask
that you may be filled with the knowledge of His will
in all wisdom and spiritual understanding.*
Colossians 1:9 NKJV

*Grow in grace and understanding
of our Master and Savior, Jesus Christ.
Glory to the Master, now and forever! Yes!*
2 Peter 3:18 MSG

*I press on toward the goal to win the prize for which God
has called me heavenward in Christ Jesus.*
Philippians 3:14 NIV

*For the LORD giveth wisdom:
out of his mouth cometh knowledge and understanding.*
Proverbs 2:6 KJV

The path to spiritual maturity unfolds day by day. Each day offers the opportunity to worship God, to ignore God, or to rebel against God. When we worship Him with our prayers, our words, our thoughts, and our actions, we are blessed by the richness of our relationship with the Father. But if we ignore God altogether or intentionally rebel against His commandments, we rob ourselves of His blessings.

Today offers yet another opportunity for spiritual growth. If you choose, you can seize that opportunity by obeying God's Word, by seeking His will, and by walking with His Son.

Be filled with the Holy Spirit; join a church where the members believe the Bible and know the Lord; seek the fellowship of other Christians; learn and be nourished by God's Word and His many promises. Conversion is not the end of your journey—it is only the beginning.

Corrie ten Boom

— A Prayer —

Lord, help me to keep growing spiritually and emotionally. Let me live according to Your Word, and let me grow in my faith every day that I live.

Amen

Strength

The LORD is my strength and my song . . . .

Exodus 15:2 NIV

But the people who trust in the Lord will become strong again. They will rise up as an eagle in the sky. They will run without needing rest. They will walk without becoming tired.

Isaiah 40:31 ICB

I am able to do all things through Him who strengthens me.

Philippians 4:13 HCSB

For I the LORD thy God will hold thy right hand, saying unto thee, Fear not; I will help thee.

Isaiah 41:13 KJV

God is our refuge and strength, a very present help in trouble.

Psalm 46:1 KJV

Where do you go to find strength? The gym? The health food store? The espresso bar? There's a better source of strength, of course, and that source is God. He is a never-ending source of strength and courage if you call upon Him.

Have you "tapped in" to the power of God? Or are you muddling along under your own power? The answer to this question will determine the quality of your life here on earth and the destiny of your life throughout all eternity. So start tapping in—and remember that when it comes to strength, God is the Ultimate Source.

God is the One who provides our strength,
not only to cope with the demands of the day,
but also to rise above them.
May we look to Him for the strength to soar.

Jim Gallery

— A Prayer —

Dear Lord, I will turn to You for strength.
When my responsibilities seem overwhelming,
I will trust You to give me courage and perspective.
Today and every day, I will look to You as the ultimate
source of my hope, my strength, my peace,
and my salvation.

Amen

Temptation

The Lord knows how to deliver the godly out of temptations.

2 Peter 2:9 NKJV

This High Priest of ours understands our weaknesses, for he faced all of the same temptations we do, yet he did not sin.

Hebrews 4:15 NLT

No temptation has seized you except what is common to man. And God is faithful; he will not let you be tempted beyond what you can bear. But when you are tempted, he will also provide a way out so that you can stand up under it.

1 Corinthians 10:13 NIV

Yet in all these things we are more than conquerors through Him who loved us.

Romans 8:37 NKJV

Blessed is the man who endures temptation; for when he has been approved, he will receive the crown of life which the Lord has promised to those who love Him.

James 1:12 NKJV

If we are to avoid the unending temptations of this world, we must arm ourselves with the Word of God.

In a letter to believers, Peter offered a stern warning: "Your adversary, the devil, prowls around like a roaring lion, seeking someone to devour" (1 Peter 5:8 NASB). What was true in New Testament times is equally true in our own. Satan tempts his prey and then devours them. As believing Christians, we must beware. And, if we seek righteousness in our own lives, we must earnestly wrap ourselves in the protection of God's Holy Word. When we do, we are secure.

Do not fight the temptation in detail. Turn from it.
Look ONLY at your Lord. Sing. Read. Work.

Amy Carmichael

— A Prayer —

Lord, life is filled with temptations to stray from
Your chosen path. But, I face no temptation that
You have not already met and conquered through
my Lord and Savior Jesus Christ,
the One who empowers me with His strength
and His love.

Amen

Thanksgiving

Finally, brethren, whatsoever things are true, whatsoever things are honest, whatsoever things are just, whatsoever things are pure, whatsoever things are lovely, whatsoever things are of good report; if there be any virtue, and if there be any praise, think on these things.

Philippians 4:8 KJV

Thanks be to God for His indescribable gift.

2 Corinthians 9:15 HCSB

And let the peace of God rule in your hearts . . . and be ye thankful.

Colossians 3:15 KJV

In everything give thanks;
for this is God's will for you in Christ Jesus.

1 Thessalonians 5:18 NIV

I will praise the name of God with a song,
and will magnify him with thanksgiving.

Psalm 69:30 KJV

Every good gift comes from God. As believers who have been saved by a risen Christ, we owe unending thanksgiving to our Heavenly Father. Yet sometimes, amid the crush of everyday living, we simply don't stop long enough to pause and thank our Creator for His countless blessings.

As believing Christians, we are blessed beyond measure. Thus, thanksgiving should become a habit, a regular part of our daily routines. God's gifts are too numerous to count, and we owe Him everything, including our eternal praise . . . starting now.

The ability to rejoice in any situation is
a sign of spiritual maturity.

Billy Graham

— A Prayer —

Lord, let me be a thankful Christian.
Your blessings are priceless and eternal.
I praise You, Lord, for Your gifts and,
most of all, for Your Son.
Amen

Today

While it is daytime, we must continue doing the work of the One who sent me. Night is coming, when no one can work.

John 9:4 NCV

Give your entire attention to what God is doing right now, and don't get worked up about what may or may not happen tomorrow. God will help you deal with whatever hard things come up when the time comes.

Matthew 6:34 MSG

This is the day the Lord has made; let us rejoice and be glad in it.

Psalm 118:24 NIV

. . . encourage one another daily, as long as it is Today.

Hebrews 3:13 NIV

. . . I know whom I have believed, and am convinced that he is able to guard what I have entrusted to him for that day.

2 Timothy 1:12 NIV

When will you rejoice at God's marvelous creation? Today or tomorrow? When will you accept His abundance: now or later? When will you accept the peace that can and should be yours? In the present moment or in the distant future? The answer, of course, is straightforward: The best moment to accept God's gifts is the present one.

Will you accept God's blessings now or later? Are you willing to give Him your full attention today? Hopefully so. He deserves it. And so, for that matter, do you.

Men spend their lives in anticipation,
in determining to be vastly happy at some period
or other, when they have time. But the present time has
one advantage over every other: it is ours.

Charles Caleb Colton

— A Prayer —

Lord, You have given me another day of life;
let me celebrate this day, and let me use it according to
Your plan. I praise You, Father, for my life and for
the friends and family who make it rich. Enable me to
live each moment to the fullest as I give thanks for
Your creation, for Your love, and for Your Son.

Amen

Troubles

Let not your heart be troubled:
ye believe in God, believe also in me.

John 14:1 KJV

I have told you these things so that you can have peace in me. In this world you will have trouble. But be brave! I have overcome the world!

John 16:33 ICB

Even though good people may be bothered by trouble seven times, they are never defeated.

Proverbs 24:16 NCV

He heals the brokenhearted, and binds their wounds.

Psalm 147:3 NASB

He restoreth my soul: he leadeth me in the paths of righteousness for his name's sake.

Psalm 23:3 KJV

Throughout the seasons of life, we must all endure life-altering personal losses that leave us breathless. When we do, God stands ready to protect us.

Vance Havner had practical advice for Christian friends of every generation. He advised, "No journey is complete that does not lead through some dark valleys. We can properly comfort others only with the comfort we ourselves have been given by God." Let us use our own troubles, then, to comfort others and, by doing so, give glory to the One who first comforted us.

Looking back, I can see that the most exciting events of my life have all risen out of trouble.

Catherine Marshall

— A Prayer —

Dear Lord, You are my strength in times of adversity.
When I am troubled, You comfort me.
When I am discouraged, You lift me up.
Whatever my circumstances, Lord, let me trust
Your plan for my life. And, when my family and friends
are troubled, let me remind them of Your love,
Your wisdom, and Your grace.

Amen

Trusting God

The Good News shows how God makes people right with himself—that it begins and ends with faith. As the Scripture says, "But those who are right with God will live by trusting in him."

Romans 1:17 NCV

O LORD of hosts, blessed is the man that trusteth in thee.

Psalm 84:12 KJV

What time I am afraid, I will trust in thee.

Psalm 56:3 KJV

But it is good for me to draw near to God:
I have put my trust in the Lord GOD . . . .

Psalm 73:28 KJV

Trust in the LORD with all thine heart;
and lean not unto thine own understanding.
In all thy ways acknowledge him,
and he shall direct thy paths.

Proverbs 3:5, 6 KJV

Where will you place your trust today? Will you trust in the ways of the world, or will you trust in the Word and the will of your Creator? If you aspire to do great things for God's kingdom, you will trust Him completely.

When you trust your Heavenly Father without reservation, you can rest assured: in His own fashion and in His own time, God will bless you in ways that you never could have imagined. So trust Him, and then prepare yourself for the abundance and joy that will most certainly be yours through Him.

Ten thousand enemies cannot stop a Christian,
cannot even slow him down, if he meets them
in an attitude of complete trust in God.

A. W. Tozer

— A Prayer —

Dear Lord, I will turn my concerns over to You.
I will trust Your love, Your Wisdom, Your plan,
Your Promises, and Your Son—
today and every day that I live.

Amen

Truth

A person who does not have the Spirit does not accept the truths that come from the Spirit of God. That person thinks they are foolish and cannot understand them, because they can only be judged to be true by the Spirit. The spiritual person is able to judge all things, but no one can judge him.

1 Corinthians 2:14, 15 NCV

I have no greater joy than to hear
that my children walk in truth.

3 John 1:4 KJV

Teach me Your way, O LORD; I will walk in Your truth.

Psalm 86:11 NASB

For there is nothing covered, that shall not be revealed; neither hid, that shall not be known. Therefore, whatsoever ye have spoken in darkness shall be heard in the light; and that which ye have spoken in the ear in closets shall be proclaimed upon the housetops.

Luke 12:1, 3 KJV

And ye shall know the truth,
and the truth shall make you free.

John 8:32 KJV

The words of John 8:32 are both familiar and profound: The truth, indeed, will make you free. Truth is God's way: He commands His children to live in truth, and He rewards those who follow His commandment. Jesus is the personification of a perfect, liberating truth that offers salvation to mankind.

Do you seek to walk with God? Do you seek to feel God's peace? Then you must walk in truth, and you must walk with the Savior. There is simply no other way.

Having a doctrine pass before the mind is not what the Bible means by knowing the truth. It's only when it reaches down deep into the heart that the truth begins to set us free, just as a key must penetrate a lock to turn it, or as rainfall must saturate the earth down to the roots in order for your garden to grow.

John Eldredge

— A Prayer —

Heavenly Father, You are the way and the truth and the light. Today, as I follow Your way, and live in Your truth, and share Your light with my friends, I thank You for the inevitable result in my life: freedom.

Amen

Waiting on God

Yet the LORD longs to be gracious to you;
he rises to show you compassion.
For the LORD is a God of justice.
Blessed are all who wait for him!

Isaiah 30:18 NIV

Indeed, let no one who waits on You be ashamed; . . .
For You are the God of my salvation;
On You I wait all the day.

Psalm 25:3, 5 NKJV

Be still before the Lord and wait patiently for him . . . .

Psalm 37:7 NIV

We urge you, brethren, admonish the unruly,
encourage the fainthearted, help the weak,
be patient with everyone.

1 Thessalonians 5:14 NASB

The Lord is wonderfully good to those who wait for him
and seek him. So it is good to wait quietly
for salvation from the Lord.

Lamentations 3:25, 26 NLT

Lamentations 3:25, 26 reminds us that it is good to wait quietly for God. But for most of us, waiting patiently for Him is difficult. Why? Because we are fallible human beings with a long list of earthly desires and a definite timetable for obtaining them.

The next time you find yourself impatiently waiting for God to reveal Himself, remember that the world unfolds according to His timetable, not ours. Sometimes, we must wait, and when we do, we should do so quietly and patiently. And, as we consider God's love for us and the perfection of His plans, we can be comforted in the certain knowledge that His timing is perfect, even if our patience is not.

Waiting on God brings us to the journey's end
quicker than our feet.

Mrs. Charles E. Cowman

— A Prayer —

Dear Lord, make my work pleasing to You.
Help me to sow the seeds of Your abundance everywhere
I go. Let me be diligent in all my undertakings
and give me patience to wait for Your harvest.

Amen

Witnessing

And when the Holy Spirit comes on you, you will be able to be my witnesses in Jerusalem, all over Judea and Samaria, even to the ends of the world.

Acts 1:8 MSG

We are therefore Christ's ambassadors, as though God were making his appeal through us. We implore you on Christ's behalf: Be reconciled to God.

2 Corinthians 5:20 NIV

You are the light of the world. A city that is set on a hill cannot be hidden. Nor do they light a lamp and put it under a basket, but on a lampstand, and it gives light to all who are in the house. Let your light so shine before men, that they may see your good works and glorify your Father in heaven.

Matthew 5:14-16 NKJV

. . . in your hearts set apart Christ as Lord. Always be prepared to give an answer to everyone who asks you to give the reason for the hope that you have.

1 Peter 3:15 NIV

Among the greatest gifts that we can give to our friends or family members is a willingness to share our personal testimonies. But sometimes, because we are fearful that we might be rebuffed, we may be slow to acknowledge the changes that Christ has made in our lives. Every believer, each in his or her own way, bears responsibility for sharing the Good News of our Savior. It is important to remember that we bear witness through both words and actions.

Billy Graham observed, "Our faith grows by expression. If we want to keep our faith, we must share it." If you are a follower of Christ, the time to express your belief in Him is now. You know how He has touched your heart; help Him do the same for others.

Walking with God down the avenue of prayer,
we acquire something of His likeness, and unconsciously
we become witnesses to others of
His beauty and His grace.

E. M. Bounds

— A Prayer —

Dear Lord, let me share the Good News of
Your Son Jesus. Let the life that I live and the words
that I speak be a witness to my faith in Him. And let me
share the story of my salvation with others so that
they, too, might dedicate their lives to Christ
and receive His eternal gifts.

Amen

Work

*Be strong and brave, and do the work.
Don't be afraid or discouraged, because the Lord God,
my God, is with you. He will not fail you or leave you.*

1 Chronicles 28:20 NCV

*But thanks be to God, who gives us the victory through our
Lord Jesus Christ. Therefore, my beloved brethren,
be steadfast, immovable, always abounding in the work of
the Lord, knowing that your labor is not in vain in the Lord.*

1 Corinthians 15:57, 58 NKJV

*But let every man prove his own work, and then shall
he have rejoicing in himself alone, and not in another.
For every man shall bear his own burden.*

Galatians 6:4, 5 KJV

*But this I say, He which soweth sparingly shall
reap also sparingly; and he which soweth
bountifully shall reap also bountifully.*

2 Corinthians 9:6 KJV

The old adage is both familiar and true: We must pray as if everything depended upon God, but work as if everything depended upon us. Yet sometimes, when we are weary and discouraged, we may allow our worries to sap our energy and our hope. God has other intentions.

Are you willing to work diligently for yourself, for your family, and for your God? And are you willing to engage in work that is pleasing to your Creator? If so, you can expect your Heavenly Father to bring forth a rich harvest.

> Ordinary work, which is what most of us do
> most of the time, is ordained by God every bit
> as much as is the extraordinary.
>
> *Elisabeth Elliot*

— A Prayer —

Lord, let me be an industrious worker in Your fields.
Those fields are ripe, Lord, and Your workers are few.
Let me be counted as Your faithful,
diligent servant today, and every day.
Amen

Worship

Worship the Lord your God and . . .
serve Him only.

Matthew 4:10 HCSB

But seek first the kingdom of God and His righteousness,
and all these things shall be added to you.

Matthew 6:33 NKJV

I was glad when they said unto me,
Let us go into the house of the LORD.

Psalm 122:1 KJV

But the hour is coming, and now is, when the true
worshipers will worship the Father in spirit and truth;
for the Father is seeking such to worship Him.
God is Spirit, and those who worship Him
must worship in spirit and truth.

John 4:23, 24 NKJV

All the earth shall worship You And sing praises to You;
They shall sing praises to Your name.

Psalm 66:4 NKJV

All of mankind is engaged in the practice of worship. Some choose to worship God and, as a result, reap the joy that He intends for His children. Others distance themselves from God by worshiping such things as earthly possessions or personal gratification . . . and when they do so, they suffer.

Today and every day, God deserves your worship, your prayers, your praise, and your thanks. And you deserve the joy that is yours when you worship Him with your prayers, with your deeds, and with your life.

Worship is not taught from the pulpit.
It must be learned in the heart.

Jim Elliot

— A Prayer —

Heavenly Father, let today and every day be a time of worship. Let me worship You, not only with words and deeds, but also with my heart. In the quiet moments of the day, let me praise You and thank You for creating me, loving me, guiding me, and saving me.

Amen